MMINS • STEVEN CURRY • BENJAMIN DAVIS • DIANA DAY • PETER DeMASTER • CASTINE DEVEROUX • SHEILA DRIVER • TYLOR
ES • ASHLEY MEGAN ECKLES • SUSAN JANE FERRELL • CHIP FIELDS • KATHERINE FINLEY • JUDY FISHER • LINDA FLORENCE •
NALD FRITZLER • MARY ANNE FRITZLER • TEVIN GARRETT • LAURA GARRISON •

DSON • KEVIN
" GOTTSHALL II • ETHEL GRIFFIN • JURETTA GUILES • RANDY GUZMAN • CH   D HARDING •
OMAS HAWTHORNE Sr • ADELE HIGGINBOTTOM • ANITA HIGHTOWER • G   O • COLLEEN
USLEY • GEORGE HOWARD • WANDA LEE HOWELL • ROBBIN HUFF • CHARLES HUR   DOUGLAS ICE •
RISTI JENKINS • NORMA JEAN JOHNSON • RAYMOND JOHNSON • LARRY JONES • ALVIN JUSTES • BLAKE RYAN KENNEDY •
ROLE SUE KHALIL • VALERIE JO KOELSCH • CAROLYN KREYMBORG • TERESA LEA LAUDERDALE • KATHY LEINEN • CARRIE ANN
Z • DONALD LEONARD • LAKESHA LEVY • DOMINIQUE LONDON • RHETA LONG • MICHAEL LOUDENSLAGER • DONNA LUSTER •
ERT LEE LUSTER Jr • MICKEY MARONEY • BRENDA DANIELS MARSH • J.K. MARTIN • GILBERTO MARTINEZ • JAMES McCARTHY •
NETH McCULLOUGH • BETSY McGONNELL • LINDA McKINNEY • CARTNEY JEAN McRAVEN • CLAUDE MEDEARIS • CLAUDETTE
EK • FRANKIE ANN MERRELL • DERWIN WADE MILLER • LEIGH MITCHELL • JOHN CLAYTON MOSS III • TRISH NIX • JERRY LEE
KER • JILL RANDOLPH • MICHELLE ANN REEDER • TERRY SMITH REES • MARY RENTIE • ANTONIO REYES • KATHRYN RIDLEY
DY RIGNEY • CLAUDINE RITTER • CHRISTY ROSAS • SONJA SANDERS • LANNY SCROGGINS • KATHY LYNN SEIDL • LEORA LEE
LS • KARAN SHEPHERD • CHASE SMITH • COLTON SMITH • VICTORIA SOHN • JOHN THOMAS STEWART • DOLORES STRATTON •
LIO TAPIA • VICTORIA TEXTER • CHARLOTTE THOMAS • MICHAEL THOMPSON • VIRGINIA THOMPSON • KAYLA MARIE
SWORTH • RICK TOMLIN • LARUE TREANOR • LUTHER TREANOR • LARRY TURNER • JULES VALDEZ • JOHN KARL VANESS III •
NNY WADE • BOB WALKER Jr • DAVID WALKER • WANDA WATKINS • MICHAEL WEAVER • JULIE MARIE WELCH • ROBERT
STBERRY • ALAN WHICHER • JOANN WHITTENBERG • FRANCES WILLIAMS • SCOTT WILLIAMS • W. STEPHEN WILLIAMS •
RENCE WILSON • SHARON WOOD-CHESNUT • RONOTA WOODBRIDGE • TRESIA JO WORTON • JOHN YOUNGBLOOD • LUCIO
MAN Jr • TERESA ALEXANDER • RICHARD ALLEN • TED ALLEN • BAYLEE ALMON • DIANE ALTHOUSE • REBECCA ANDERSON •
ELA ARGO • SANDY AVERY • PETER AVILLANOZA • CALVIN BATTLE • PEOLA Y. BATTLE • DANIELLE NICOLE BELL • OLETA BIDDY •
LY TURNER BLAND • ANDREA BLANTON • OLEN BLOOMER • LOLA BOLDEN • JAMES BOLES • MARK BOLTE • CASSANDRA
KER • CAROL BOWERS • PEACHLYN BRADLEY • WOODY BRADY • CYNTHIA BROWN • PAUL BROXTERMAN • GABREON BRUCE •
BERLY BURGESS • DAVID BURKETT   JOE CARRILLO • RONA LINN CHAFEY •
KARY CHAVEZ • ROBERT CHIPM   CHRISTOPHER COOPER II • ANTONIO
ARA COOPER Jr • DANA COOPER   OVERDALE • ELIJAH COVERDALE • JACI
COYNE • KATHY CREGAN • RICH   NA DAY • PETER DeMASTER • CASTINE
EROUX • SHEILA DRIVER • TYLO   L • CHIP FIELDS • KATHERINE FINLEY
Y FISHER • LINDA FLORENCE •   ARRETT • LAURA GARRISON • JAMIE
NZER • MARGARET GOODSON •   GUILES • RANDY GUZMAN • CHERYL
DLEY HAMMONS • RONALD H   TTOM • ANITA HIGHTOWER • GENE
GES Jr • PEGGY HOLLAND •   HOWELL • ROBBIN HUFF • CHARLES
RLBURT • JEAN HURLBURT • PAU   NSON • RAYMOND JOHNSON • LARRY
ES • ALVIN JUSTES • BLAKE RYA   CH • CAROLYN KREYMBORG • TERESA
LAUDERDALE • KATHY LEINEN   EVY • DOMINIQUE LONDON • RHETA
NG • MICHAEL LOUDENSLAGER   ARONEY • BRENDA DANIELS MARSH •
MARTIN • GILBERTO MARTINE   Y McGONNELL • LINDA McKINNEY •
RTNEY JEAN McRAVEN • CLAUD   ELL • DERWIN WADE MILLER • LEIGH
CHELL • JOHN CLAYTON MOSS   CHELLE ANN REEDER • TERRY SMITH
S • MARY RENTIE • ANTONI   UDINE RITTER • CHRISTY ROSAS •
JA SANDERS • LANNY SCROGG   SHEPHERD • CHASE SMITH • COLTON
TH • VICTORIA SOHN • JOHN   A • VICTORIA TEXTER • CHARLOTTE
MAS • MICHAEL THOMPSON •   TOMLIN • LARUE TREANOR • LUTHER
ANOR • LARRY TURNER • JULES   WALKER Jr • DAVID WALKER • WANDA
KINS • MICHAEL WEAVER • JUL   R • JOANN WHITTENBERG • FRANCES
LIAMS • SCOTT WILLIAMS • W.   D-CHESNUT • RONOTA WOODBRIDGE •
SIA JO WORTON • JOHN YOUN   CHARD ALLEN • TED ALLEN • BAYLEE
ON • DIANE ALTHOUSE • REBEC   LLANOZA • CALVIN BATTLE • PEOLA Y.
TLE • DANIELLE NICOLE BELL   BLANTON • OLEN BLOOMER • LOLA
DEN • JAMES BOLES • MARK BO   BRADLEY • WOODY BRADY • CYNTHIA
WN • PAUL BROXTERMAN •   TT • DONALD BURNS • KAREN GIST
R • MICHAEL JOE CARRILLO • RONA LINN CHAFEY • ZACKARY CHAVEZ • ROBERT CHIPMAN • KIMBERLY CLARK • PEGGY CLARK •
HONY CHRISTOPHER COOPER II • ANTONIO ANSARA COOPER Jr • DANA COOPER • HARLEY COTTINGHAM • KIM COUSINS •
ON COVERDALE • ELIJAH COVERDALE • JACI RAE COYNE • KATHY CREGAN • RICHARD CUMMINS • STEVEN CURRY • BENJAMIN
IS • DIANA DAY • PETER DeMASTER • CASTINE DEVEROUX • SHEILA DRIVER • TYLOR EAVES • ASHLEY MEGAN ECKLES • SUSAN
E FERRELL • CHIP FIELDS • KATHERINE FINLEY • JUDY FISHER • LINDA FLORENCE • DONALD FRITZLER • MARY ANNE FRITZLER •
N GARRETT • LAURA GARRISON • JAMIE GENZER • MARGARET GOODSON • KEVIN "LEE" GOTTSHALL II • ETHEL GRIFFIN •
ETTA GUILES • RANDY GUZMAN • CHERYL BRADLEY HAMMONS • RONALD HARDING • THOMAS HAWTHORNE Sr • ADELE
GINBOTTOM • ANITA HIGHTOWER • GENE HODGES Jr • PEGGY HOLLAND • COLLEEN HOUSLEY • GEORGE HOWARD • WANDA
WELL • ROBBIN HUFF • CHARLES HURLBURT • JEAN HURLBURT • PAUL DOUGLAS ICE • CHRISTI JENKINS • NORMA JEAN JOHNSON •
MOND JOHNSON • LARRY JONES • ALVIN JUSTES • BLAKE RYAN KENNEDY • CAROLE SUE KHALIL • VALERIE JO KOELSCH •

IN THEIR NAME

Oklahoma City:
The official commemorative volume

EDITED BY **CLIVE IRVING**

———

PHOTOGRAPHIC AND EDITORIAL ARCHIVE
DONATED BY **THE DAILY OKLAHOMAN**

———

ORAL HISTORY ASSIGNMENT EDITOR **MIKE BRAKE**

———

PHOTO EDITOR **SUZANNE HODGART**
DESIGNER **WYNN DAN**
GRAPHICS BY **JOHN GRIMWADE**
SPECIAL COMMENTARY BY **TOM BROKAW**

Library of Congress Cataloguing-in-Publication Data is available.
ISBN 0-679-44825-X

Manufactured in the United States of America
24689753
FIRST EDITION

IN THEIR NAME

Dedicated to the brave and the innocent
Oklahoma City, April 1995

RANDOM HOUSE   NEW YORK

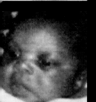

Foreword by the Rev. Billy Graham

I WILL NEVER FORGET

Few events in recent memory have burned themselves into the hearts and minds of the American people as deeply as the tragic and senseless bombing in Oklahoma City on April 19, 1995. The image of that gaping wound ripped in the side of the Alfred P. Murrah Federal Building will be indelibly imprinted on our memories as long as we live.

But also imprinted on our memories will be our pictures: a fireman tenderly cradling a dying baby; a wife frantically seeking information about a missing husband or child; emergency workers from all over America risking their lives as they struggle to find survivors; lines of people volunteering to give blood; a packed arena of people gathering for a prayer service.

I will never forget standing before the unbelievable devastation of that building. How could such a frightening thing happen? I also will never forget the privilege of meeting (along with President and Mrs. Clinton and Governor and Mrs. Keating) some of the families of the victims. My tears mingled with theirs as we talked and prayed, for this was not only a heartbreaking event for them, but for all Americans. The prayer service (which was the inspiration of Mrs. Cathy Keating) was one of the most memorable experiences of my life.

This book not only chronicles what happened during those sad days. It also is a moving tribute to the courage and faith of the people of Oklahoma City and the state of Oklahoma, almost all of whom were touched personally by the loss of someone they knew. This volume will also remind us of the selfless dedication of all who shared in the rescue effort and the tireless leadership given by Governor Keating, Mayor Norick, and so many others.

As we remember those who died in this tragedy, may we each be challenged to renew our faith, and inspired to reaffirm our commitment to banish hate and violence from our lives and our nation.

CONTENTS

All the personal accounts in this story were volunteered, drawn from more than a thousand survivors, rescuers, medical staff, counselors, volunteers, and children.

THE LAND RUSH
Pressure to open up Indian Territory to white settlers came from the "Boomers"—frontiersmen who, for a decade or more, staged repeated, illegal incursions. When Congress authorized the first Land Rush in 1889, Oklahoma City was founded. These riders were part of the fourth Land Rush, in 1893.

BIRTH OF A CITY

Over the horizon, a dream

SETTLED IN AN AFTERNOON

Before there was a state, there was a city, where the
smart could make a quick fortune

It was not, any longer, the lawless West. The only shot that was fired at high noon on April 22, 1889, came from a starting pistol. Some fifty thousand people—men, women, children—lined up to claim their piece of the new American frontier. They waited with their horses, wagons, and dreams at the boundary of the so-called Unassigned Lands.

The pistol shot began the great Land Rush, authorized by Congress only the previous month. One of the first across the line on horseback was William McClure, a rancher who had run vast herds of longhorns across this land for years.

McClure had set his sights on a railroad watering stop called Oklahoma Station, on the north bank of the North Canadian River. He had arranged a chain of hired hands with fresh horses along his route, and arrived thirty minutes ahead of the pack, in time to claim 160 acres northwest of Oklahoma Station, as well as two town lots. The rules were that any man or woman over the age of twenty-one could claim 160 acres of open land, or if more than one person entered a 320-acre site with the intention of establishing a town, they could divide it into town lots. In the impudent spirit of the times, Oklahoma City was born in an afternoon. Within two weeks the first streets and buildings were in place around the original railroad depot. The new settlers came from the drought-plagued states of the Midwest, like Iowa, Ohio, Indiana, and Illinois. Oklahoma City was a glimpse of the new century in embryo: the first police chief made a quick fortune in real estate, banking, and oil (oil was found in 1897 at Bartlesville, 161 miles from Oklahoma City).

As yet, there was no state of Oklahoma. The 69,919 square miles that would eventually constitute the state appeared on contemporary maps as Indian Territory. Over the course of several decades, many Indian tribes, caught in the path of white settlement, had been forcibly resettled into the area ("Oklahoma" was a fusion of two Choctaw Indian words—*okla*, "people," and *humma*, "red").

In 1907, Oklahoma became the forty-sixth state of the Union. At around the same time, Will Rogers, a young adventurer from Oolagah, Oklahoma, was inventing a maladroit Wild West act that eventually brought him celebrity as the ultimate cowboy sage. Rogers became the state's favorite son (Oklahoma City's airport is called the Will Rogers World Airport), and he never forgot his roots: "By golly, I am living now," he said. "I am eating real biscuits and real ham and cream gravy. Oklahoma will show the world how to live yet."

THE COWBOY SAGE
Will Rogers, as seen in the
Will Rogers Museum, painted by
Charles Banks Wilson,
circa 1992.

IT'S NOT A MIRAGE, IT'S A CITY
Three weeks before a photographer climbed to get this shot, the only thing here was a desolate railroad watering stop, Oklahoma Station. Now, on May 16, 1889, a city already has its roots down. Present downtown Oklahoma City, including the site of the Alfred P. Murrah Federal Building, is within a mile of this spot.

But it was oil, not ham and gravy, that scented the air of Oklahoma City. By the late 1920s a boom overran the city. Even the State Capitol and the Governor's Mansion were swallowed in a forest of rigs. But the boom turned to bust. Wells had been tapped too fast, and in the Depression demand slumped. This crisis was compounded by a disaster of biblical scale. In the early 1930s a succession of severe droughts helped to turn part of the Great Plains into the Dust Bowl. The land had been over-grazed, the crops lost rooting topsoil, and spring winds generated "black blizzards," the scoured dirt darkening the sky. There were forebodings that a permanent desert was in the making.

Nothing has left a deeper mark on the Okla-homan psyche, or a more lasting image of the state, than the "Okies," the desperate home-steaders who fled to California, immortalized in John Steinbeck's masterpiece *The Grapes of Wrath*. However, as the novel became a block-busting best-seller in 1940, the cycle of droughts ended. Oklahomans felt they had been fortified in spirit by being so tested, and soil-conservation programs—plus the rains—put farmers back into business. And, as in the rest of America, World War II jump-started Oklahoma's economy. By the early fifties Oklahoma City seemed the epitome of Middle America as Norman Rockwell might have pictured it. If the rest of America hardly knew where the city was, Oklahomans didn't much mind. There was a comforting security in not being conspicuous; it suited their character. And for boosterism, they could always fall back on Will Rogers: "Plenty of ranches here as big as Germany or France. Horse pastures as big as England."

A FOREST OF GUSHERS
Oil was first discovered in Oklahoma at Bartlesville, 161 miles from Oklahoma City, on April 15, 1897. This is the Tonkawa oil field in the 1920s. Prospectors hit a gusher within the city limits of Oklahoma City on December 4, 1928. The wildcatters overproduced and had to be checked as world oil prices slumped.

S.E. CORNER L. ENDICOTT

NO. 5. SEC 2 T 24-R1W NOBLE CO OKLA.

THE "OKIES": REFUGEES OF THE RED PLAINS

In 1938 Dorothea Lange found this homeless family on a road in Oklahoma. She was photographing the ravaged farmlands at the same time that John Steinbeck was writing *The Grapes of Wrath*. Lange's husband, Paul Taylor, who traveled with her, wrote, "Oklahoma is the most windblown state in the country, its newly-broken red plains are among the worst eroded..." Nonetheless, the droughts ended and farming rebounded.

A CITY OF THE HEARTLAND

Early in 1995, the largest employers in Oklahoma City were the state and federal governments. The Alfred P. Murrah Federal Building (named for a distinguished circuit-court judge), sitting at the center of this aerial view, housed sixteen agencies, employing more than five hundred people in all. Like other Middle American cities, this one was seeking ways to reenergize its economy. The downtown area is notable for the number of parking lots— there is no surge of new sky-scraper construction. The city covers a huge area, 608 square miles, and developers have no need to pay for expensive air space. Its population is young (median age 32.4 years) and three-quarters white. (From the time of the Land Rushes, Native Americans in Oklahoma gravitated to the cities, and today Oklahoma has an integrated and urbanized Native American population.)

The largest single employer is Tinker Air Force Base, in the southeastern suburb of Midwest City. The Federal Aviation Administration has a large center at the Will Rogers World Airport, and another airport, Wiley Post, was named after the aviator who died with Rogers on an Alaskan flight in 1935.

The city is well endowed with medical resources. Among the twenty hospitals are several with specialized skills, including emergency and trauma medicine. Oklahoma City sits in "Tornado Alley" and its emergency services, four police precincts, and thirty-three fire stations have been drilled in dealing with large natural disasters.

THE LAST HOURS OF INNOCENCE

Six people with a destination in common: a downtown building

By Ann DeFrange, of The Daily Oklahoman

The carpool arrived at Rick Tomlin's home at 6:00 A.M., Wednesday. When Rick got into the car, the driver pulled out onto the rural state highway near his house, then picked up a major thoroughfare to take the four government employees to downtown Oklahoma City. Rick hadn't been with his co-workers and co-passengers since the previous Friday. He and his wife, Tina, had spent the Easter holiday in St. Louis, then drove through heavy rain to get home late Monday. Rick had decided to sleep late Tuesday morning.

But Wednesday, April 19, he went over in his mind the work waiting in his office at the U.S. Department of Transportation in the Alfred P. Murrah Federal Building. Matters had to be cleared up before he hit the road again Thursday for the DOT regional office in Fort Worth. The morning was cool and cloudy, an Oklahoma City

April day that could turn into any kind of weather. Temperatures in the seventies were predicted, but elsewhere in the state, towns were conducting the annual spring ritual of cleaning up after severe windstorms. Drive-time talk radio focused on the first one hundred days of Governor Frank Keating, whose ride in on the Republican election sweep promised new directions for the state government. Legislators debated such issues as tax cuts for bingo parlors and state funds for veterans' benefits.

The top story of the day, though, was the renovation of downtown Oklahoma City that had captured the imagination and excitement of its citizens. Dreams of river canals, professional-sports facilities, arts complexes, and hotels were finally coming true. After a decade of spiraling boom-and-bust economics, residents had made a desperate move toward recovery. They voted for a sales tax that would finance the $285 million Metropolitan Area Projects plan. Tuesday, the City Council had haggled over construction contracts for a minor league baseball stadium just east of the downtown business district. It was a pleasant problem. Today, though, city leaders and the Governor started their morning at the Myriad Convention Center, about five blocks from the Federal Building. They convened at 6:45 for a popular annual event, the Metropolitan Oklahoma City Prayer Breakfast, co-sponsored by Mayor Ron Norick. The 1,200 guests included the Mayor, Governor Keating, lieutenant governor Mary Fallin, district attorney Bob Macy, and police chief Sam Gonzales. Gathered over sausage and eggs, biscuits and gravy, were representatives of nearly every major corporation and public utility in the area, and other civic and religious leaders. The breakfasters passed the first of the anticipated 11,000 guests scurrying to open the Midsouthwest Foodservice Convention in another part of the Myriad and then settled in to listen to a motivational speaker pump them into a new resolve to put their religion into their workdays. The guests spoke of how great it was in Oklahoma City, and how much better it would be when the renovation was complete.

The prayer breakfast adjourned at 8:30, and most of the public officials and business leaders of Oklahoma City were soon back on the streets and on their way to their jobs.

Pamela Argo was up this morning, as every morning, at 4:00 A.M. She sometimes arrived at work by 5:00 A.M. If she could log on to her computer in the Quality Resources Management and Utility Review Department at Presbyterian Hospital before the doctors arrived, her work went so much faster. In that hour between rising and leaving home she was locked into her usual

efficient routine, which revolved around her animals. Most were strays that Pam had found and carried home. The three cats sat in the bathroom while she showered—white Neige and black Samson and orange Pumpkin settling into their regular spots on the windowsill or the sink or the edge of the bathtub. Pam carried on conversations with them while she dressed.

On April 19, she chose a typical outfit—black skirt, long black tunic shirt, black mesh hose, her big black bag, and a black hat. She had a conversation, too, with a cousin's daughter. Lindsay Harris, ten, who adored Pam because they did grown-up "girl things" together, phoned. Pam promised to be at her next soccer game.

Reticent, quiet Dr. Charles Hurlburt let his exuberant wife, Jean, lure him into retirement activities that kept them almost as busy as the careers they hadn't quite left. He went with her to cake-decorating classes, and she convinced him they should both be Red Cross volunteers. They had recently completed training so they could assist in potential disasters. But retirement also meant paperwork and red tape. Early on April 19, they took Jean's Social Security papers and left the house.

Tuesday evening, Scott and Sharon Coyne sprayed their home for fleas, and thinking it would be safer for them and their only daughter, fourteen-month-old Jaci Rae, they went to spend the night at Sharon's mother's home. Both families lived in Moore, a suburb south of Oklahoma City. Jaci woke during the night, confused in the strange surroundings. Scott answered her distress call; in the morning, Sharon found the two of them curled up on a small sofa, Jaci nestled between her daddy and the sofa pillows.

She was a morning baby. "Arms up!" her mother said, and Jaci's hands flew high to slip through petite sleeves. Mother and baby played hide-and-seek with tiny fingers as they adjusted her clothing—a new outfit this morning, shorts and a baby-doll shirt with roses. Sometimes they sang together. Jaci's favorite was "Itsy Bitsy Spider," and she could almost—but not quite—make the shapes with her fingers.

Pete DeMaster had an office at the Murrah Building and another at Tinker Air Force Base. But he spent a lot of time on the road, collecting personal-background information on people who applied for top-security clearances from the Department of Defense. He usually drove from home to Tinker and picked up a government car, but Pete had a new vehicle of his own, a 1995 silver Oldsmobile. He drove straight downtown to the Murrah Building, leaving at the same time as his wife, Karen, who tried to beat the tardy bell at Northeast High School, where she was vice-principal.

Rick Tomlin was frequently on the road in his job as a motor vehicle safety officer. He developed programs, supervised inspections, and worked with highway patrol divisions as well as private trucking operations. Rick, forty-six years old, was a conscientious government employee. Signs of waste rankled him. His arrival at the Federal Building at 6:45 A.M. gave him fifteen minutes to start the coffee pot; he was the only coffee drinker in his office, so he believed he shouldn't brew on "government time." That integrity pervaded his life. Though he was eligible for exemption, he had joined the navy for the Vietnam War, seeing it as an American duty. His new wife, Tina, waited for him at home in Kansas.

DOT transferred them and their two sons around the country. They had arrived in Oklahoma City four years ago from North Carolina, and picked a house in a development of large lots near Piedmont, a bedroom community west of Oklahoma City. That location provided not only a small school system for the sons they were raising with a strict respect for law and morals, but also the privacy they wanted. The neighborhood gave Rick room for his hobbies, too. He raised cactus and joined a local garden club. He restored classic cars. He was proud of the shed he and his sons had just finished making to shelter their works in progress.

Rick and Tina were rarely able to talk on the phone when he was out of town, so they made the most of the opportunity when he was office-bound. Tina, who worked in a photo processing lab at Glamour Shots, called him when she took a break precisely at 9:00 A.M. This morning, he looked forward to the call.

Dr. Charles Hurlburt retired six years ago from the University of Oklahoma College of Dentistry, where he had taught radiology to freshman students for the previous sixteen years. Jean Hurlburt retired as a registered nurse at Deaconess Hospital, but worked as many hours as Social Security would allow and saved her money for the travels they were learning to enjoy. They'd already been around the world, but not for vacations.

Charles was raised by missionary parents in the Belgian Congo. At age twenty-four, he came back to the United States to study dentistry at Wheaton College, in Illinois. There he met Jean, a nursing student. He and Jean went back to Africa for a ten-year medical mission. But with two small daughters and another born in Africa, it was a difficult time for Jean. She was relieved when they moved to the University of Oklahoma job in the early 1970s. Jean loved nursing, and she was the image of a classic nurturing nurse. The staff at Deaconess was well aware that she checked out, then frequently sneaked back into the hospital in the evening to sit with troubled patients.

In contrast to his wife's energy, Charles was a quiet, humble man. He had a pacemaker, but he drove people to medical appointments and visited hospital shut-ins, and he didn't talk about what he did. She learned to paint china plates, advancing from flowers to houses and scenery. He took care of the pool. Together, they gardened, creating a children's garden for their nine grandchildren.

They took senior-citizen bus tours. Jean loved them, and spent hours before the trips putting little verses, puzzles, and cartoons in envelopes to entertain strangers on the bus. They flew to Israel and cruised the Caribbean. Their next trip was to be to San Antonio, on April 21.

Sharon and Jaci Coyne went downtown together every day. Sharon worked in the Federal Court Clerk's office, and her fourteen-month-old daughter, Jaci, stayed in the day-care center in the Murrah Building. With Sharon's sister employed by the U.S. Marshals Service and many family friends throughout the government offices, they joked about being a "federal family" and Jaci's future as a U.S. Attorney. Jaci had her own small rituals. She liked to throw her bottle out the car door as soon as Sharon opened it; sometimes Sharon crawled around on the garage floor in her office clothes to retrieve it. Jaci was learning to climb the steps from the garage by herself, a four-inch struggle. She pushed the elevator button and carefully manipulated the intimidating step at the entrance.

If her mother helped her, she could ring the bell at the day-care center door. This morning she rang it twice. Her favorite teacher, Miss Brenda, greeted her. Miss Brenda called her Miss Jaci. Jaci didn't cry when Miss Brenda picked her up.

Pete DeMaster planned for a career in the air force, and he was stationed with an AWACS unit at Tinker Air Force Base near Oklahoma City when he was divorced. More than the air force, he wanted custody of his daughter, Kristin, then nine years old. He left the military as a captain and joined the Department of Defense as an investigator. Fatherly activities took him one day to a neighborhood swim party, and there he met Karen, who lived two houses away from him. She was raising a son, Brian, a year younger than Kristin. They married thirteen years ago.

A new stepson delighted Pete for several reasons, one of which was that it gave him access to the Boy Scouts again. His father had been a leader, Pete became an Eagle Scout, and the kind of kids scouting attracted were kids Pete liked. But even after Brian announced he wasn't interested in scouting, Pete stayed an avid scout leader. And, his friends teased him, a "perpetual Eagle Scout." Pete still dressed like the ROTC officer he once was. He had a quick smile, polite manners, and an unflappable temperament.

His emotions were let loose for only two causes—hockey games, which he attended faithfully at the Myriad Convention Center, and Karen, whom he loved. They would celebrate their thirteenth wedding anniversary on April 24. Their tradition was dinner out and a dozen red roses. Conservative Pete believed red roses and red jewelry fit Karen, and she was already expecting a new red stone to match the garnets and rubies on her Victorian slide bracelet.

Pam Argo, thirty-six, still had family in Stigler, pop. 2,500, in eastern Oklahoma. She left there the day after high school graduation, but her close family ties held. Her parents, Billy and Joyce Cleveland, a sister, grandparents, numerous cousins and aunts and uncles and even more distant relatives still gathered at Stigler, and wherever they were needed. Bossy Pam kept the annual family reunions organized.

Pam's dad traveled frequently to Oklahoma City to work on Pam's sixty-year-old brick house. The new fence was almost finished. Pam's sister had visited the week before; the two of them planted 150 gladiolus bulbs to replace the 150 tulips that had already peaked.

Pam Argo's bad moods were as dramatic as the good ones. Life wasn't always easy for her, and her family's support had been important on many occasions. She and her husband, Tomy, had separated four years ago. They hadn't divorced, because he was ill and she continued to carry him on her insurance policy; sometimes she helped nurse him. Tomy died in March, and Pam took a much-needed vacation to Puerta Vallarta.

Her favorite color was black. From two hundred hats she picked one to wear to work each day in windy Oklahoma, where hats are not a fashion staple. Her free spirit, in fact, was kept in control by a rigid sense of order. Pam was compulsively organized at every level of her life. Black clothing hung in order on black hangers; the white items, on white hangers. Her silverware had to be turned all in one direction.

The huge weekly calendar that sat on her desk listed her activities in detail. She penciled in a year's worth of birthdays and anniversaries ahead of time. Clipped to the Mother's Day page was the envelope holding pre-purchased tickets for an ice skating show. The square for April 19 showed that her car insurance was due, that a friend needed a ride from the airport at 3:00 P.M., and that she had to complete paperwork for Tomy's burial benefits. For that last chore, she had made an appointment at the Social Security office at 9:00 A.M.

Just before 9:00 A.M., Pete DeMaster called a DOD agent in Lawton for some information. The agent promised to call him back in ten minutes.

Pam Argo complained to her co-workers about having to go to the Social Security office; she had hoped to conduct the business by phone or mail. She decided to take a taxi the mile from the hospital to downtown.

"I'll be back in ten minutes," she announced.

Just after 9:00 A.M., a Social Security employee stepped into the waiting area and called Pam's name. Another worker looked out the first floor window and noted aloud that a woman dressed in flashy black clothes—readily recognizable as Pam—had left a cab and was walking up the steps.

Sharon Coyne dropped the diaper bag in its place and handed Jaci over to the day-care teacher. "Mama's got to go to work," she told her daughter.

She kissed her goodbye, and said, "I love you." Jaci smiled her answer.

The Hurlburts were fortunate. They found a parking spot for their Toyota van right at the corner of the Federal Building at Fifth and Harvey. At 9:00 A.M., they were standing in line in the Social Security office, holding Jean's papers.

When she took her nine o'clock break, Tina Tomlin immediately called her husband. They chatted. She wanted him to know she had made it to the photo lab safely. Rick confided his concern about the work that had piled up during his days off. Over the phone, Tina heard a loud noise. The line went dead. It was 9:02.

From KFOR

9:02 A.M.

"Explosion downtown! Some kind of explosion. We need help..."

THE KILLING FIELD
Seen soon after the blast from Tinker Air Force Base, twelve miles away, Oklahoma City looks like any Middle American capital: trees, before a sudden skyline.

RESCUER BECOMES VICTIM
Rebecca Anderson collapsed outside the Federal Building after trying to pull people free. She suffered a fatal head injury from falling debris and was the only outside rescuer to die.

All the people Officer Terrance Yeakey (left) helped to rescue survived; after falling into a hole in the crater, he himself ended up in the hospital.

The first report of an explosion came from a police patrol car in the downtown area. Within seconds, the police and fire department radio channels erupted with calls. All over Oklahoma City people felt the force of a blast. Some thought it was a sonic boom; others a gas explosion. Those who were trained to respond to an emergency—doctors, nurses, police, firemen—dropped whatever they were doing and tried to find out if they were needed. Some heard radio reports; others saw the first live television pictures. As police and firemen located the site of the explosion, the scale of the devastation astounded them. Nobody comprehended the cause, but the carnage was clear and terrible on the streets. The focus was the block framing the Alfred P. Murrah Federal Building—between Fourth and Fifth streets, east to west, and Harvey and Robinson, north to south. When rescuers converged on this area, they found what they later recalled as "organized chaos." Within a pattern of trained responses, hundreds of individual acts of heroism and initiative—dealing with grim life-or-death decisions—were carried out in the first hour. What follows are the accounts of survivors of the blast and those who formed the impromptu rescue and medical teams. Their own words are interspersed with flashes from the police and fire department radio channels.

Clark C. Peterson was at work in his office on the fourth floor of the Murrah Building at 9:02:
At about 8:58 A.M., I sat three feet from the north windows as my supervisor gave me final instructions for a project. I returned to my desk, which was about twenty feet south of the windows, and began to type. At about 9:02 A.M., an electric spark appeared by my computer and everything turned black. Propelled objects raced throughout the darkness amid the sound of moaning metal.

I caught a glimpse of a terrified girl with both arms straight up in the air. We were apparently falling, but I did not realize what had happened until a minute or two later. The sight of her was so brief and faint that I could not identify her. She yelled, "Ah!" as if there were not enough time to inhale air.

I was calm throughout; everything changed to a deadlike settling of debris amid the black atmosphere. As the blackness and dust began to clear, I discovered that the armchair I was seated in had been replaced. I remained in a sitting position, but on a flat, ceilinglike material, which was on top of a three-story pile of rubble.

I saw the north half of the Murrah Building was gone, except for the east and west sides. I was ten feet in front of the remaining structure, about level with the third floor. "This had to be a bomb!" I thought, and a twenty-foot crater below confirmed that it was. I could not see anybody else in the building or rubble.

POLICE (unknown unit): An explosion downtown! Some kind of explosion! We need help!

Sergeant Jerry Flowers is with the Oklahoma City Police Gang Unit. He was one of the first on the scene:
At 9:02 A.M. I was in the Police Academy discussing training. The academy building shook. Major Steve Upchurch yelled down the hallway that the Federal Building downtown had just blown up. Sergeant Steve Carson, Sergeant Don Hull, and I put on our police raid jackets. I drove to Fourth Street close to Hudson, where we were forced to stop because of debris. We ran toward the Murrah Building. Black smoke was shooting in the air. People, both old and young, were covered with blood. Some were holding towels and

clothing articles against their bodies trying to stop the bleeding. Babies and adults were lying on the sidewalks. Some appeared to be dead and some alive. Everywhere I looked was blood, misery, and pain. One lady sat on a curb holding a blood-soaked shirt against her head while a stream of blood ran down her chest. What touched me about her was that she was trying to console a small girl, about eight years old, whose hair was matted with blood and gray dust. I've never seen so much pain, both physical and emotional.

Steve Carson and I ran to the north side of the Federal Building. I saw a car hood burning in the top of a tree. Debris, rocks, bodies, burned cars, glass, fire, and water covered Fifth Street. A large hole about thirty feet in diameter was where a small circle drive used to be in front of the Murrah Building, used by handicapped motorists. As we approached the northwest corner of the building, I could see a small hole where rescue workers were going into the building. Sergeant Bob Smart with the OCPD Robbery Detail was yelling, "Let's get these people out." Steve and I ran into the rubble and were handed a board stretcher that had a middle-aged man on it. He was covered with blood and his clothes were mostly torn off. It was obvious that he was dead. We passed this man to the outside of the building. I never saw him again.

Rhonda Griffin was at work in the HUD office on the seventh floor of the Federal Building:
I arrived at work at 8:45 A.M. My area was at the southeast end of the Federal Building, I saw Betsy and we said good morning to each other. I signed in and went to my desk (it faced west). I sat down, placed my purse in my desk drawer, and turned my computer on. Michael walked past me and we said good morning to each other. (Michael shared a cubicle with me.) I got up from my desk and

started down to the west end of the floor; it was 8:52 A.M. I saw Kim at her desk, and I said, "Good morning, Kim!" I will never forget the big smile on her pretty face. I arrived at Rita's desk and she was not there. I asked her supervisor, Bob, if she would be back soon, because I needed her to notarize papers. He told me that she was in training on the ninth floor. I noticed that he was the only one in his area and jokingly asked him why everyone had deserted him. He told me that some were in training and some were in the field. The last thing he said to me that morning was, "Rhonda, you have a good day." I started back to my desk and had only taken a few steps when I saw Rita. We walked back to her desk and she notarized the papers for me. She told me that she had to hurry because she had to be in training in six minutes. As we parted we decided on lunch at the normal time, 12:15. It was unusually bare at HUD that day. There were around sixty people out on both the seventh and eighth floors.

At about 9:00 A.M. I walked to my desk and sat down, then placed the notarized papers in an envelope. I started to get up and take it to the mail tray when I heard something go SWOOOOOOOOSH and everything went gray. I thought my computer had blown up so I threw my arms and hands over my face and head and rolled my chair back with my feet (eastward) to get away from my computer. I started feeling things hitting me and I thought, "Oh my God, the computer has blown the ceiling down." Things kept hitting and I began to think that maybe I had fallen asleep at my desk and was having a bad nightmare. Then again, maybe I had lost my mind! Finally it stopped. When I opened my eyes I was at Glenda's workstation, still sitting in my chair. (Her station is about four feet behind mine.) Glenda was standing there. She had not even sat down at her desk when the bomb exploded. I

EYE OF THE STORM
Minutes after the blast, smoke
from a parking lot was still
drifting into the gaping hulk of
the Federal Building. Both victims
and rescuers were choking on
smoke and thick dust. Lieutenant
Dennis Griffin checked the
parking lot for victims.

stood up and looked at where my desk and Michael had been. They were no longer there. About three feet above where I had been sitting before I went backward, was a huge concrete slab dangling, held only by a piece of rebar.

Glenda said that I asked, "What's happening to us? Our building is gone and we are still here." I remember thinking that it was a bomb and that it was worse than the one at the World Trade Center. Smoke surrounded us and we could not breathe. We thought that the building was on fire. Glenda raised her skirt up and we put it over our mouths and noses. I remember saying that if we can get to the window, we can breathe. We made our way to the windows and looked out.

POLICE: ...bring all fire and ambulances you can get...

Sergeant Jerry Flowers: Steve and I went through a small door. The floor went drastically downhill. Water came up over the top of my boots and the dust nearly prevented us from breathing. It was very dark as we crawled over large pillars of concrete just to get to an area where we could hear people yelling for help. We made our way into a room where large slabs of concrete were lying from one floor down to the next. There was a large hole you could look up through and see the nine broken floors hanging above our heads. Large ropes of steel rebar hung down and others protruded from the floor where we were trying to walk.

People were yelling for help. Our vision was impaired by darkness and dust. One lady was imprisoned under a huge slab of concrete and rebar, yelling to rescue workers not to leave her. I reached between the rebar and rock, patting her back and telling her we would get her out. Firefighters swarmed into the room. A generator was

started and portable lights lit up the area we were in. As firefighters started to cut the steel to free the woman, we heard another cry. Looking down into what appeared to be a well, we saw a lady trapped on her back by concrete. The floor around her was filling up with water. She kept yelling, "Don't let me drown." Rescuers attacked the well to free the woman and were successful.

Dr. Carl Spengler, an emergency-room physician at University Hospital, had driven with a student paramedic to the site:
Except for a distant building alarm and a circling helicopter, the area was so quiet we could hear the birds singing. As the debris fell, it echoed through the street. A fireman said, "Doc, you may want to go check the guy down there in the bomb crater." I stood and stared blankly at the thirty-foot-wide, twelve-foot-deep hole. I made my way down to the person at the bottom. He had been killed from a fall or a crush injury. There was a blood-streaked trail where he had slid off a large slab of concrete above and rolled into the crater. As I climbed out of the crater, I saw two men lying just above the slab of concrete. As I made my way up to the men, I lost my balance and fell over one of them lying on his back. I ended up almost face to face with him, and it was obvious that he had been crushed. The second man was partially buried facedown. It was clear that if I did not get off the rubble pile, I stood a good chance of being buried myself. On my way up, I found one more victim who had met the same fate.

Clark C. Peterson: I wondered, "How can I still be alive when five floors of concrete above collapsed, leaving nothing but air and the sky above?" My answer: God's angels had to be protecting me. I moved closer to the pillars, then

SOUND EFFECTS
While cars burned outside the Federal Building, those trapped inside could hear gas tanks and tires exploding.

climbed on top of another pile of rubble, which was also topped by a flat piece of material. The first people to arrive on the street below saw me bloodied and showered with dirt, in a short-sleeve striped shirt, brown pants, and white shoes. A man yelled, "Sit down!" With my mouth full of dust, it was hard to project, but I said, "There's a crack on this board and if my weight doesn't remain equalized, the board might break and I'd fall several floors. Others need help more than I do. Help them. I can stand here a long time."

Then, several muffled cries for help came from a woman, possibly from under the debris of the third or fourth floor. A fire truck's extension ladder reached to the fifth or sixth floor. Down came a man strapped to a stretcher; his upper and lower right leg appeared cut in half, except for connecting thin fibers of skin.

After I had been standing on a pile of rubble for about thirty minutes, two men appeared and each grabbed one of my wrists. I was pulled up to the fourth floor and was directed to get immediate medical attention. An ambulance took me to Children's Hospital, where Dr. Tyson found multiple injuries. Cuts, scrapes, and bruises covered most of my head, hands, arms, and legs, including lacerations that required fourteen stitches. My lower back muscles took the brunt of my fifteen-foot fall when I landed in a sitting position. The muscle pain ceased only a week after the blast. Due to weightlifting, my lower back took the fall quite well, and possibly prevented a broken back. My three fellow office workers are gone—Karen Carr, Peggy Holland, and John Moss. An excavator said that their deaths were not painful, but instantaneous. According to his assessment, their crushing deathblows lasted one two-hundredth of a second.

Leroy Tatom is the helicopter pilot for KWTV: We were airborne within five minutes of the explosion and approached the Murrah Building from the north-northwest. We couldn't see the damaged north face due to smoke from burning cars. We began transmitting a live picture back to the station. I think it was this first picture of the scene that got people's attention.

One police helicopter was already circling. We remained high enough to stay clear of it and the downtown buildings. When we got around to the northeast side of the building, we had our first clear view of the destruction. We could not believe so much of the building was blown away. Buildings in Beirut look like this, not Oklahoma City.

POLICE: ...it appears this explosion was at the Federal Building, not the courthouse...

Rhonda Griffin: Everything was so still. Then we started seeing people running toward the building and people coming out. The next thing I remember seeing is the bomb-squad truck, fire trucks, police cars, ambulances, people crying and screaming as they were being helped from the building, people covered in blood, people unconscious (or maybe lifeless).

We realized we could not get to the stairs to get out because the bomb had blasted a hole from the north to the south side. I thought that what was left of the building was going to collapse. I kept screaming, "Somebody help us!" We started praying. We prayed for everyone who had been in the building. Then I remembered the day-care center, and I said, "The babies!" We prayed for them. We prayed for ourselves.

Several rescuers refer during this account to a basement in the Federal Building. There was no basement: *The first floor, where the Social Security offices were, was at ground level, linked to an underground parking garage on the south side. Water was rising as victims were found trapped there. Richard Dean, who escaped from the Social Security office on the first floor and returned to look for survivors, discovered that an eight-inch pressurized pipe that provided "chiller water" for the air-conditioning system was severed and was pouring water into the debris. The water was cold, about forty-two degrees. Dean called a firefighter, but it took another twenty minutes to get the water turned off. By then the crater outside the building had filled up, with a layer of debris floating on the top.*

Sergeant Jerry Flowers: Firemen yelled down to us from above to take hold of a stretcher. We lowered a lady whose injuries didn't appear to be too bad. I thought this lady for sure would survive, but learned later that she died. I saw another person on her back trapped between two large slabs of concrete. Firefighters did manage to free this lady and she was taken out of the building. A fireman brought us some paper masks to wear so we could breathe. The smell in the dark, water-soaked room was musty and stale. I shined my flashlight over my head and could see the crushed victims between the floors. Dark, thick blood leaked through the cracked layers of concrete, marking the place of yet another body. As rescue workers worked furiously to free these trapped people, a fireman yelled for us to get out. Another bomb had been found, bigger than the first. We looked at each other, thinking about how we could leave these people trapped in here, but were told a second time to get out. The screaming voices of the trapped people kept telling us not to leave them. It was hard, but as far as I know, we all vacated the crumbling building as ordered.

POLICE: …I've got three injured down…make that five down….

Rhonda Griffin: There was a second bomb scare. Everyone was ordered to evacuate the building. A rescue worker told us to lie down on the floor. We tried, but there was too much glass. I remember kneeling with my head under my arms. Then something said to me, "What are you doing on the floor? If the building blows up, you will die whether you are on the floor or standing. Stand up so they can see you." I stood back up, and so did Glenda. I looked out the window and thought that if I had to stay in this building, I would die— if I jumped, maybe I'd live. I asked Glenda if she wanted to jump. She said, "No." I was still contemplating whether to jump or not when I turned my head and there stood a man. (I met him a few days later and he said that something told him that if he didn't get to us, we would jump.) He risked his life and disobeyed orders by coming into the building. He risked his life again when he tested the window frame by walking across to us. He took us by the hands one by one and walked us over the frame to the other side. He took me first and I stood there while he got Glenda over. I wasn't leaving that building without her. Two police officers took us by the hand as we ran down the stairs and out from the building. It was 10:35 A.M.

Raymond Washburn, who has been blind since childhood, managed the Federal Building's fourth-floor snack bar for seven years:
One of my two employees called in sick. Kim Wallace prepared sandwiches as usual and I ran the register. Kim went on break at 8:45 A.M. in front of the building. I sent her fifteen minutes earlier than I normally do. When she came back, I told

MISSING PIECES "I looked down and in the middle of the street I saw an axle," said a witness. "There was no car around and I thought, 'Where is the car that belongs to this axle?'"

her I needed to make a deposit at the credit union. I waited on another customer, and as I turned around, something hit me on the shoulder and head. At first I thought it was a piece of ceiling tile, but it got heavier and pushed me down where all the debris was on my feet. I could only lift them a couple of inches. I heard Kim hollering that she couldn't get up. I said I couldn't get to her, but I'd meet her at the door.

I started to the door, where the counter had been, but it was no longer there. The customer I had just waited on said we needed to start toward the back, to the kitchen, where we found Kim. She had been thrown to the floor. Every morning I stick my cane in the corner of the kitchen. I reached for it, but it was not there. The customer led me out with Kim. We exited on the stairs at the southwest end of the building, and as soon as we did, the floor in the snack bar dropped. We made it to the patio area. A sheriff asked if I was hurt. I had cuts on my elbow. Kim had a cut on her leg. They took me to the hospital and bandaged me up.

I wish there were more lucky ones. I knew just about everyone in the building. I knew the children; they came to the snack bar sometimes. I heard people screaming below me in the building. That sticks in my mind. Counseling has helped me talk it out. I still have my bad days—especially Wednesdays. I ask a lot, "Why us?"

That's one day I was glad I couldn't see.

Brad Lovelace is a police officer with the Oklahoma Capital Patrol. Within minutes of the explosion, he began searching the YMCA Building, to the northeast of the Federal Building:
I came to a room that terrified me. Although it was damaged extensively, I could tell that fifteen minutes earlier it had been a functioning day-care center. Thoughts of my two small daughters rushed through my head. I yelled out, "Is anyone in here?" I found nothing and heard no one, so I moved on and at approximately 9:30 A.M., my efforts were rewarded. In the corner of the basement, I saw three little girls huddled up together. They were obviously in shock and could not speak. I told them they were going to be fine and asked them their names, but it seemed as though they were not even listening. The girls were between ages four and six. They were too big for me to carry all three upstairs at once, so I picked up the two smallest girls and told the eldest that I would be right back to get her. Immediately, her daze was gone and tears welled up in her eyes. I got down on my knees, at face level with her, and said, "I promise I'll be back." She nodded. I carried the two smaller girls up the stairs and out to the triage center. When I returned to the basement, the older girl was still in the same spot waiting for me. When she saw me, she said nothing and didn't smile, but put her arms out toward me. I picked her up, carried her out, and went back to the YMCA to finish my search.

POLICE: ...assembling walking wounded, fire department's first aid station is at Fifth and Broadway...

Shane Davidson is a corporal with the Oklahoma City Fire Department. He was on duty at Fire Station One, five blocks west of the Federal Building, on the morning of April 19. He arrived at the site less than one minute after the bombing:
We found a badly injured child on the first floor, got it out, and continued to search for those whose screams we could hear. On the second floor, I helped remove several severely injured children from a pile of rubble at the west end of the building. As I pulled these small children from the

FALSE ALARM
Medical assistants Janet Froelich (left),
Wilma Jackson, and Kerri Albright
fled the Murrah Building, in fear of
a second bomb, when rescuers
were ordered to leave trapped
survivors as they tried to free them.

A VIEW OF HELL CALLED TRIAGE

"I tagged them minor, I tagged them moderate, I tagged them critical, and if they were not breathing, I tagged them dead."

Heather Taylor is a college student majoring in basic emergency medical technology. She arrived early at the scene with Dr. Carl Spengler:

My adrenaline was the only thing that was keeping me going, because I hadn't slept for twenty-four hours and I didn't realize how serious the situation was. I heard some people screaming, and ran over to this man who looked just like my grandfather. The man had severe lacerations on his scalp and neck, from falling glass. He was still breathing and was awake. He was shaking, a sign of shock. Dr. Spengler checked his lung sounds and yelled real loud, "Take a deep breath."

I left Dr. Spengler to see about a police officer who had fallen. He

College student Heather Taylor and Doctor Carl Spengler

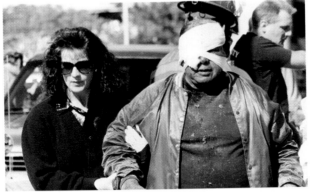

was lying on the ground, screaming that his back was burning. EMSA trucks began to arrive, but I was the only trained rescue worker there. I grabbed a C collar. I was yelling at the cop to hold still, since he probably had a cervical-spinal injury. I placed the collar on him. Someone got a long spine board and we strapped him to it and an ambulance took him away.

I realized that I didn't have any personal protective equipment on, and the scene was not safe and secure. We are taught that paramedics are not useful if they are dead paramedics. So I grabbed some gloves and gave some to the doctor. While I was putting them on, I looked up and saw a man walking on what was left of the third floor. I told Dr. Spengler that we needed to get him down because he was missing his right arm. While the fire department worked to get him down, we decided to see what the other side of the building was like.

The south side of the building was the worst. Dr. Spengler decided we needed to set up the triage (an area where victims are given priority according to their condition), since no one else was doing it. More and more people started to arrive with the equipment we needed. This was the moment when I got scared. Dr. Spengler gave me triage tags and told me to follow him around and tag the people minor, moderate, critical, or dead. You would think that you wouldn't waste your time on the dead, but tagging the dead kept people from going back to them and trying to save them.

On the curb outside the building, the wounded were lined up. If they were talking, I tagged them minor; if they were bleeding severely, I tagged them moderate; if they were unconscious, I tagged them critical; and if they were not breathing, I tagged them dead.

As the firemen were bringing out the wounded, I tagged the first child dead. I heard someone tell me there was once a day care on the second floor. After that, I found myself making a temporary morgue—some call it "the church." A priest had arrived, and he followed right behind me, praying for the lost ones. The firemen were bringing out so many dead. As soon as I would take one child, another child was laid next to it. I remember one man, a bystander who was helping me, said, "Why all of the children, why?" I just watched him cry.

In the streets, brutal decisions about saving lives.

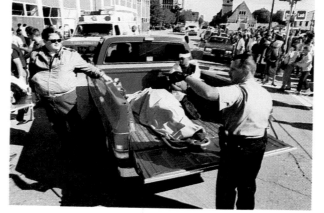

Then I heard the doctor calling my name, so I went to him. They had pulled a lady from the rubble. She was unconscious, she was missing her left foot, her right hand had been amputated, and her mandible was crushed. As Dr. Spengler was intubating her (putting a breathing tube through the mouth into the lungs), I was writing everything down and tagged her critical.

I went to the next victim pulled from the rubble, a woman in her twenties. She was unresponsive. I had been told that she was pregnant. As I was tying her down to the long spine board, I noticed that both of her legs had been crushed severely. After I tagged her, she was transported. Later I heard that she had died.

Our first priority was to establish a triage team. Dr. Spengler got on the intercom of the fire truck and told everyone to listen. I was amazed at how he took charge of the situation and everyone listened to him. He told everyone that he wanted twenty paramedics, twenty physicians, and twenty ICU nurses. He looked at me and said that I was to stay with him wherever he went. I just nodded.

Dr. Spengler instructed the firemen to let me tag all the victims coming out of the building. Since most of the victims brought out of the building were dead, I just made the tags out to read "Dead—Dr. Spengler," then I signed my initials. About six more dead children were brought out. I said a little prayer for them as I tagged them.

I will never forget my experience with this horrible tragedy. As I start my career in emergency medicine, nothing I will do will ever compare. I did learn I can make a difference.

LOCAL HEROES
The Oklahoma City Fire Department rescued all the survivors save one—and handled, too, most of the dead. "They were our people," said special operations chief Mike Shannon.

COLLATERAL DAMAGE
Barry Fogerty lived.
Two of his colleagues
at the Water Resources
Board, right across the
street from the Federal
Building, died.

debris, they were so covered in blood and dust, it was impossible to tell if they were girls or boys, black or white. They were children, and we were thankful they were alive.

After getting the children out, I sort of went on automatic pilot. I found a police officer trying to reach a woman buried in the rubble. We could hear her crying for help and we spent thirty minutes digging with our hands to reach her. She kept asking us to find her husband and tell him that she loved him. We told her that she could tell him herself when we got her out. We reached her and had freed her right arm when the order came to evacuate the building because of the possibility of a second bomb. The policeman, an FBI agent, and I decided to stay and try to get the woman out. We decided after about ten minutes, though, that we needed some heavy equipment and more manpower. We explained to her why we were leaving and promised to return quickly. Once outside, however, we were prevented from reentering the building. The order agonized us. We had promised the woman we would return for her, and we felt we had let her down.

The woman was Priscilla Salyers, who worked in the U.S. Customs Office on the fifth floor. She takes up the story:
Suddenly someone took my hand. Words cannot begin to express the comfort and peace I felt with this human touch. I could hear several men working around me. They kept talking to me and reassuring me everything was going to be okay. Then, the man holding my hand said, "Priscilla, we have to leave." I begged him not to leave me and he told me again they had to leave.

After what seemed like hours, I could hear movement and I began throwing rocks and rubble and making as much noise as possible with my arm. I heard a man yell, "There's a live one, get over here!" Suddenly I felt someone take my hand and realized this man had been talking about me. I could hear men talking about the problems of getting me out. The man holding my hand asked me my name. Several times he asked me my name and it was taking so much energy to take a deep breath to answer. I became very frustrated and remember thinking: "Forget my name, just keep digging!" Every time I heard someone ask him if I was alert and doing okay, I squeezed his hand very hard. There was no way I wanted this man to leave me and I wanted him to know I was very alert. It seemed to be taking forever, but I still had confidence in these men and tried to be patient. They worked very hard and I knew they were tired and worn out, but they never slowed down. They used the chains and the "jaw" and were able to release me from the rubble. They flipped me over and the first thing I saw was the sky. I was shocked. I turned to my left and saw firemen climbing over cement slabs and rubble. It looked like a war zone. Looking up, I saw face after face after face and every one of them was talking to me and encouraging me to hang in there, that I would be okay. They placed me in the ambulance and paramedics drove me to St. Anthony.

Corporal Davidson saw Priscilla Salyers later in the hospital. She told him she understood why he had to leave her. She had three broken ribs, a punctured and collapsed lung, and other minor injuries.

POLICE: ...when they come in this building, bring flashlights!

Sergeant Jerry Flowers: We waded out of the dark hole we were in and made our way back to the same entrance we had used about an hour earlier. Several intense minutes passed while we waited for a second explosion. When nothing happened, Don Hull and I went to the south side of the building. The damage was not as bad, but was still viewed as deadly. Injured people were being treated by emergency-services personnel on the buckled sidewalk in front of the building. I could see a man sitting in what used to be a window. He seemed to be looking out at the crowd. As I got closer to him, I realized that both of his legs were gone below his hips. He was obviously dead.

Don and I went into the building and immediately got separated. A few minutes later, Don came back to the front opening where I was. He was carrying a small baby wrapped in a blanket. We laid the baby on the front sidewalk just outside the building. A nurse put a piece of tape around the ankle of the child. Don opened the blanket to wrap it better. That is when I saw that the child was decapitated. I wondered why and how in God's name this could happen. Cradling the baby in his arms, Don carried it to emergency-services workers and then rejoined me in the building to continue the search. In a small area cluttered with rocks and steel, I saw the tiny pink foot of a child. Altogether, five children were carried from this area of the second floor.

Luckily, Fifth Street was not a canyon of glass-walled towers. Directly opposite the Murrah Building and Ground Zero was a parking lot. This helped dissipate the shock wave on the north side. But the gas tanks of parked cars blew up, creating the impression of secondary explosions, and car tires blew from the heat (in the Federal Building, some survivors thought, mistakenly, that ammunition stored in the ATF offices was exploding). On the north side of the parking lot was the Journal Record Building, where, at 9:02,

Susan Urbach was in her office on the third floor:
My office looked out on the Federal Building. I had just made coffee and was standing talking to June, a training consultant. Brian, a staffer, was in his office, and Janet, another staffer, was in the training room on the third floor mezzanine.

All of a sudden the office literally exploded. I saw not only the suspended ceilings come down but the plaster ceiling and walls coming down, and I was knocked to the ground on my right side, so that my left side took the full force of all the falling rubble. My first thought was that I just needed to get up and get out. My arms were above my head and it was very awkward, but I was able to get everything off me and climb out. I didn't stop to look back to check anything, or even try to find my shoes, which were no longer on my feet. Brian, June, and I headed for the door, walking over several feet of rubble that used to be our office. The top of my suit was all the way open—I no longer had any buttons on my clothing.

We headed out into the hallway and met the staffers from the State Historical Preservation Office, who were next door, and started down the stairway, which was also in rubble. The marble wainscoting had fallen off and was lying cracked in the hallway. There was a great deal of smoke and fumes, and I was worried that we might suffocate. There was no hysteria, no screaming, and the only shouting was for everyone to keep to the right and let the injured come through first. They kept letting me go through; I did not know I was hurt. I felt some blood on my face, and when I put my hand against the wall for support, I saw it was completely bloody, but I felt nothing. Brian went ahead, trying to kick away as much glass as he could from my bare feet.

It was minutes after the explosion when we reached the street, and the ambulances were already there. As soon as we got out of the building we saw Janet, so I knew all my staff was out. It was a cool morning, and a woman gave me her sweater and a man kneeled next to me to shield me from the wind. June had some injuries, and someone covered us with a blanket. The medical personnel taped a compress to my neck and back and I lay in the street while they started filling up their ambulances.

I was lying next to Polly Nichols, who heads the Oklahoma Foundation for Excellence, whose office was down the other side of the hall from me. Her staff had carried her down and she had a cut jugular vein and trachea. I held her hand before they took her off. I think shock is a wonderful thing for the body. I felt nothing. I could see this huge lump of plaster in my arm and hand and couldn't feel it. I knew I was bleeding now quite profusely from my neck and back, but I couldn't feel it. Polly knew how hurt she was and was scared, but she wasn't feeling, either.

I took some pretty good hits: my ear was almost in two; my left elbow took the most jagged cuts and the dirtiest plaster and concrete; but my back was the worst, having taken the full force of the glass.

As survivors in the Federal Building regained their senses, several realized that only inches separated them from precipitous ledges. They shouted warnings to each other. In what remained of the fifth floor, on the western end where the Veterans Administration was, Stan Rombaun was in a precarious situation and John Colvin came to his aid:

Rombaun: I have a vague recollection of hearing a whooop! sound and then a sensation of strong wind. The next thing I knew I was lying on the floor to the right of my desk, next to a window that was now gone. A couple more feet and I would've been

over the edge. I felt dizzy and confused. I raised my left hand and saw it was covered with blood. My fingers were pointing every which way. Then I realized my head was also bleeding. I called out, "Somebody help me, will you?" John Colvin called out, "Stan, don't move. I'm coming to get you."

Colvin: I jumped over desks and trash to make my way to Stan, who was at the northeast window. He was within a foot or two from falling out the fifth floor. I knew I had to get him away from the edge of the building. Stan is a big fellow, so with his help I pulled him about twenty to thirty feet inside. He said, "John, I cannot go any further." I told him to relax as much as possible.

Rombaun: I had curled into a fetal position by the time he got to me and started pulling me from the window. He managed to get me up, but I slipped and fell. He said, "I'll be right back." A minute later he returned with another co-worker, then some other people came into the area. Somehow they led me to the hallway, where I buckled to the floor again. My vision was impaired, so I wasn't able to comprehend the extent of the destruction.

Colvin: I met someone in a blue uniform and told him where Stan was. Within fifteen minutes, Stan was down on the south side of the building by my side. After I helped load people into ambulances for about an hour, I walked south on Harvey, without a shirt on. Some man asked me if I was cold and I said yes. He gave me the tweed jacket off his back. Then I went about two more blocks and asked a lady if I could use her phone to call my wife. She let me use the phone and then took me home.

Tim Giblet works in the Oklahoma County Assessor's Office. After helping in several areas, he found himself in the day-care center:
It was dark and difficult to see, but we uncovered the body of a young black woman. I knelt down

and held her left hand with my left hand and checked for a pulse with the fingers of my right hand. I noticed the beautiful wedding band she was wearing and how the diamond sparkled and shone as though it were a small light. To this day, I don't know where that light was coming from. This woman will never know, and her family may never know, how that scene changed my life. As I was holding her hand, I thought of my wife and how much I loved her, and I promised God that never again would I fail to hold her, praise her, or tell her how much I loved her when the thought came to me, because the husband of this woman would never get the chance again to hold her and express how much she meant to him.

THE CHILDREN SPARED
Sheriff's deputy Michael Valleen (right) carries his own son, Desmond, to safety, but "every adult standing there had a child in his or her arms," said a witness outside the Downtown YMCA Child Development Center.

In the northeast corner of the building, the site of the day-care center, police sergeant John Avera had helped rescue two women. He and Sergeant Dan Helmuth returned inside and heard a baby crying:

Avera: To my surprise, we found two babies. It was so dark, we could not tell the race of either. Officer Helmuth picked up his baby and started out of the building. I picked up my baby and started out of the building through the parking garage. I could not find any life signs. I thought the left leg and arm were broken. I carried my baby to the first firefighter I saw. He pointed to the ambulance. I ran toward this ambulance and was met by Captain Chris Fields, who had his arms outstretched. I told him I had a critical baby and wanted him to care for it. [The baby was Baylee Almon; the handover became iconic of the disaster—see page 58.]

Helmuth: The second child was a small black child, wearing a diaper and T-shirt. He had stopped crying but appeared to be alive, with a bleeding head wound. I cradled him in my arms, and as I stumbled back across the rubble pile, my left arm brushed against metal that was in contact with live electrical line and I received a shock. I jerked away and ran upstairs with the child. As I came out onto the plaza, a plainclothes deputy sheriff came running up with arms outstretched and I gave the child to him. The child, P. J. Allen, survived.

POLICE: Headquarters! We need a ladder to the southeast corner of the Federal Building.

One of the few rescues seen on television was that of Jack Gobin from the fifth floor, on the eastern end of the building. He tells the story:
Three of us, my secretary Cindy King, Dr. Brian Espe, and I, looked to the north and saw the gaping hole that had been our office. We were standing on a piece of concrete, roughly twenty percent of our floor area, a small shelf hanging from two

wall sections five stories up. I remember Dr. Espe saying, "My entire staff is gone!" We were cut off from the stairway. We yelled down through the south windows that we were not seriously injured but could not get down. A security guard or policeman, I don't remember which, arrived by climbing along the south window ledge. He stayed with us until the firemen were able to get their truck close enough to extend the ladder.

The fire dispatch radio center was only five blocks west on the same street as the Federal Building. The phone system had locked up during the early minutes, but the fire and police operators coped.

FIRE: I have Truck 5 settin' up their aerial ladder in the corner of the Federal Building...

Clinton G. Greenwood is assigned to the Oklahoma City Fire Department's Truck 5:
We backed the truck in, only feet away from the thirty-foot bomb crater. My officer, Bart Everett, climbed up first. He brought down the first victim, the woman. She was shook up pretty bad, but extremely happy to see us. It was my turn next. The floor the victims had been on was not more than fifteen feet wide and twenty-five feet long. "Who's next?" I asked. If it wasn't for the situation, it would almost have been funny. Everyone looked at each other and didn't say a thing. Finally, the man closest to me, Jack Gobin, volunteered. I backed down a couple of rungs so Jack could board. I told him just to take his time. He kept asking if this ladder could really hold both of us. I said, "This is state-of-the-art equipment. The city paid big bucks for this truck. This is your taxpayer's dollars at work." I don't know if that made him feel better or not, but afterward he said he would never gripe about high taxes again.

Children were still being found in the ruins of the day-care center. Don Hull, a homicide detective, spotted a small foot and leg and then dug out a child. At first, he thought the child was not breathing:
The child's left arm was folded behind his body. He had a compound fracture about two inches below his shoulder, but he was not bleeding, not even from the very large laceration on the left of his face. I gently moved his arm around his body to where it belonged. The child gasped and began to cry and then began to bleed badly. I folded his arm across his chest and put my hand over the cut on his face and pressed it back together. I picked him up and pressed his arm and face against my chest to attempt to slow the bleeding. The others requested that I hand the child down the line as we had done with other children, but I was unable to do this. I feared his arm might not withstand the transfers. I held the small boy tightly to my body and slowly made my way to the entrance.

As I reached the top of the rubble blocking the entrance, I was worried that the child was not breathing, but then he began to cry. I moved toward the medical teams. Twice in the short space between locations, the child again stopped breathing and required CPR and responded each time. I heard a woman's voice yelling, "That's my baby, that's my baby." I saw from the corner of my eye a man and woman running toward me. I was terrified that a mother should see her child like this and feared that he might not survive and this would be her last memory of him. I turned my back and prevented her from seeing the child. I found medics and told them of the child's condition. The mother continued trying to get to the child and wanted to know how he was. I told the mother that her child would be all right but that he needed to go to a hospital now. I carried the child to the rear of a waiting ambulance. He again stopped breathing. His head fell back and his eyes rolled into his head. I again began CPR and begged the child to breathe and again he responded.

The child was twenty-month-old Joseph Webber. He went into intensive care at Children's Hospital, but six weeks later, he returned home.

Having realized the scale of injuries, Dr. Carl Spengler had set up a triage site at the southwest of the Federal Building, enlisting an emergency medical trainee, Heather Taylor (see her story on page 46). Dr. Spengler faced an ugly moment:
Some people brought out a little girl who was still breathing. Nurses were preparing IVs. The crowd was screaming for the doctors to work on the child. I finally yelled for everybody to shut up. As I assessed the little girl, it was obvious she had catastrophic head and chest injuries…there was nothing left to save. I told a paramedic to get a blanket, wrap the child, and do nothing. People screamed, "You bastard." I stepped back and said, "Let her die." Another physician also stood up and said, "She's dead already." As I walked off, several of the people continued to curse me. That's the nature of triage: In an emergency situation, you concentrate on the ones you can save and sacrifice the ones who are beyond help. It can be very tough, but it saves lives.

Major Vernon Simpson is a veteran of the Oklahoma City Fire Department:
We found a woman in the basement who had been on the third floor. She was wedged in a little hole with her rear on one level and her head below. She was in that position for six hours. She was getting nervous at one point and she said, "Tell me a joke." I said, "I don't know too many jokes. I'm a fireman. All the jokes I know are probably dirty anyway." She started getting panicky, and I patted her hand and said, "You tell us a joke. We don't even care if it's dirty or not." She said, "Listen, for the past few hours I've had a religious experience and I ain't about to waste it on a dirty joke."

On any morning in the Federal Building there were visitors using the services. In the Federal Credit Union on the third floor, three customers were killed. Nancy Ingram went to the credit union with a deposit at 8:55:
At nine o'clock the tellers were ready, so I took care of my business and was on my way out when I stopped at the doorway to say good morning to my longtime friend Patti Hall, a credit union employee. The next thing I knew I was buried alive. I don't remember hearing a noise. I think I remember seeing chunks of concrete and ceiling panels falling like rain all around me. I must have automatically thrown my hands up over my face when I started falling, and that's what saved my life. That action formed a pocket of air that gave me space to breathe. I don't know how long I was unconscious, but I woke up yelling, "Help! Help!" and I never stopped yelling. Finally, I heard a voice say, "There are people here on the second floor." "No, we're on the third floor," I yelled. "There are people trapped here. Please come help us!" I didn't know that the third floor had fallen to the second and, in some cases, to the ground floor. I heard the rescuers climbing over twisted metal and concrete. "You're walking on my head!" I yelled. That helped them locate me and they started digging. They finally got my face uncovered, but they couldn't budge the heavy boulder lying on my legs. Two volunteer triage nurses, Trish Walker and Irene Phillips, from St. Anthony Hospital, climbed

THE ULTIMATE OUTRAGE

"I was looking through the viewfinder when suddenly a police officer appeared holding a baby in his arms"

Within twenty-four hours, one image of the bombing had become universal: the tiny, broken body of Baylee Almon cradled in the arms of firefighter Chris Fields. The picture appeared on the covers of, among many magazines, *Newsweek* and *The Economist*, as well as in scores of newspapers. The day-care center for the children of federal

workers was on the second floor of the Murrah Building. Thirty children were enrolled, but on the morning of April 19, at 9:02 A.M. only twenty-one children had been dropped there by their parents (because of a recent change in the management of the center, some parents had pulled their children out). The previous day, Baylee Almon had celebrated her first birthday.

Lester (Bob) LaRue, a safety coordinator for the Oklahoma Natural Gas Company, tells how the photo of Baylee Almon came to be taken:
I heard the blast, and after seeing the smoke billowing up, I feared a natural gas explosion. Gary Duncan and I jumped in my company vehicle and headed downtown, five miles south of my office. I parked a half-block east of Broadway, on Sixth Street. I grabbed the camera that I always kept in the car and stuffed a few rolls of film in my pockets, and we took off on foot, running west on Sixth Street. I saw people running east. They looked like they had been hit by shrapnel: people with blood-matted hair, cuts on their faces, holes and tears in clothing, seeping blood. There was no screaming.

I just noticed a hurried, quiet terror in their faces.

I was looking for Oklahoma Natural Gas employees, who would be wearing orange fire suits and white hard hats. I saw triage units being set up on Sixth. The sounds of car alarms, burglar alarms, and automobile tires and gas tanks exploding filled the air. I smelled gasoline. I spotted ONG crews and followed them as they shut off underground gas lines and large gas meters. I watched, ready to warn them if overhead rubble shifted. I took photographs as I went, and I was looking through the viewfinder when suddenly a police officer appeared holding a baby in his arms. He handed her to a firefighter. Later I learned the police officer was Sergeant John Avera, the firefighter Chris Fields, and the bloodied baby Baylee Almon. I snapped two photographs of the firefighter with the baby, but I don't remember doing it. Up to this point, I had taken no pictures of the victims, out of respect for their privacy.

Later, I dropped my film off at Moto Photo in Penn Square Mall. When I picked up the photos, an employee named Keith asked if he could keep some of the pictures to show the media. Keith showed my photos to a representative of *Newsweek*, and they wanted all the negatives, which I agreed to. The sale of these photos will allow me to contribute to the relief fund. At night I have nightmares: I dream of the victims and again I see little Baylee Almon.

up and started an IV to get my blood pressure under control. Those two beautiful girls looked like angels in blue flowing gowns. I wasn't sure if I was still buried alive or if I had died and gone with these angels to heaven. It was another half hour before firefighters brought in a hydraulic jack and wire clippers to cut me out, but the girls stayed right there with me.

Nancy Ingram's friend Patti Hall survived, with serious injuries; Nancy was in the hospital for three weeks.

In the Federal Building it remained a matter of luck whether anyone who was still alive could attract attention. The water was eighteen inches deep when police sergeant Joe P. Johnson reached the northwest corner at ground level:
Captain Bobby Lax shouted to us to remain quiet so that he could listen. After a few moments, he heard someone tapping out SOS. He shouted at the individual and assured them that we would get them out. The area where he was working was so small that the rest of us were forced to hang back. We formed a chain and began passing tools back and forth to him so that he could dig this victim out. At times we could see only his lower legs and feet. If the building had shifted, most of us wouldn't have made it out of the area, especially Bobby. Utility workers arrived and began stringing work lights and moving debris. After Bobby had extricated the victim, I saw him and the other firemen execute a very much deserved high-five. The survivor, Sheara Gamble, had been in danger of drowning, in addition to being buried alive.

Even while the rescue effort was at its most intense, the search for evidence that might lead to the source of the bomb got under way. A significant discovery was made by Sergeant Melvin Sumter, a deputy with the Oklahoma County Sheriff's Office:
At about 10:00 A.M. I joined the Oklahoma County Bomb Squad and I was instructed to take photographs of all the cars in the area and anything that could be a car, truck, or bomb part. I worked my way west on Fifth street and noticed a small red Ford parked in front of the Regency Tower Apartments. The front of the car was smashed and the windshield was broken. Lying beside the passenger front fender was a truck rear end and axle, which I photographed. After looking closer, I noticed under the dirt and grease there were some numbers. I started to rub the dirt and grease off and I realized that it was the VIN [vehicle identification number]. At 10:50, I notified special agent Norman from the FBI that I had found a VIN from a truck. I read the number to Norman and he told one of his agents to run that number. I was told three days later by an FBI agent that by noon they had found that the truck was a Ryder vehicle out of Kansas.

Sandy Teel and Robyn Parent are good friends and fellow employees of HUD:
Sandy: I thought the copier blew up. When everything stopped, I was on the floor and part of the copier was on top of me, along with all kinds of debris. I started shoving everything off me, trying to get up. When I stood up, I realized that part of the building was gone. Just four feet to the north and two feet to the east of me, everything was open—no building—and I was caught out on a ledge. There was no building left in front of me. I turned around, and the only person I could see was one of my co-workers, Larry Harris. Even though Larry worked in a different branch, I could see him because all the dividing walls were gone. I yelled to Larry and told him I was on the edge

of the building. Larry climbed over debris and grabbed my arm and helped pull me away from the edge and then Robyn started yelling at us. If I'd been at my desk I would have been hurt much worse, or killed. It was covered with debris.

Robyn: My first thought was that my computer blew up in my face—it felt like an arrow went through my left eye into my head. I was on the floor and I could not see for all the glass and blood in my face. I yelled for someone to help me, but I could hear nothing except the cars across the street exploding. I stood up and Pamela Cooper, another co-worker, said, "Robyn, don't move, don't move at all. The building is gone in front of you." For once in my life, I listened and did what I was told. I could then open my right eye enough to see that if I had taken two steps, I would have walked right off the edge of the building.

Sandy helped Robyn down the stairs, and they were discovered by paramedics on Fourth Street. Robyn suffered a concussion to the optic nerve of her left eye and had surgery for a detached and torn retina. The chances of her regaining sight in that eye were slim.

Jennifer D. Rodgers is a sergeant with the Oklahoma City Police Bicycle Patrol Unit:
On the third floor a man began yelling to me that he had found someone. He pointed across a huge hole in the center of the building and shouted, "See the arm, see the arm?" Then I saw it! I ran around the hole and ended up on the north side of the building in the middle, getting closer to a trapped man. He was lying on his stomach, with his face turned away from me. He was on the edge of the hole, with a concrete slab holding him up. Although he looked secure, the slab looked like it was about to fall to the next floor. I began working away debris from around his legs and grew more frustrated by the rebar, which seemed to be winning this war. I then caught a glimpse of a firefighter. I yelled to him to help me, and he responded. He asked me not to leave him if he fell into the hole. I promised I wouldn't. He climbed onto the slab while holding my hand. He made it safely to the other side so that he was closer to the upper body of the injured man. We continued to move debris away as a ladder truck moved closer. While I worked, I talked to the injured man. He finally moved his head and looked back at me. The right side of his face was disfigured and covered with blood. I don't even think he saw me, because I could never see his eyes. When it was time to move him, I had one piece of rebar that I could not move alone. I yelled, "I need some hands," and there they were within a second. I showed a maintenance man where to pull and together we got the man's leg free. The firefighters were then able to take the man down the ladder.

Captain Russell Burkhalter rode to the site on the back of OCFD Truck 5:
Captain Fields and I went around to the south side of the building and crawled down into the rubble. A police officer heard someone calling out from beneath the debris and we began digging. There was a woman who was able to tell us that her name was Sheila. I don't know how long we had been digging before Sheila said, "You are standing on my back!" She was not yet visible to us, so we could only determine the approximate location of her back by moving around in a circular pattern until her pain subsided. The hole we were creating was nearly four feet in diameter. Sheila told us that she was three months pregnant and feared for her child. That worried us, with the weight of all the debris and not knowing the extent of her injuries. Her hand became free and I held it for a

A RACE WITH RISING WATER
Sergeant Richard Williams (left) and Sergeant Keith Simonds (right) had to struggle through rising water and live electrical wires in near-total darkness to bring victims out from the first floor; here, they help Sharon Littlejohn, twenty-eight, a Social Security employee—and a survivor.

moment to reassure her. We cleared her face and part of a shoulder and called for oxygen. Sheila began to lose consciousness. Outwardly, she had no real signs of visible injury, but she was covered with a heavy amount of dust and insulation fibers. We knew we had to hurry. We tried to lift her out of this big hole with our hands, but her left foot was trapped. I removed some of the trash and we pulled her free. She had a badly fractured left tibia and fibula. She was lifted out of this terrible place alive!

Sheila Driver, a twenty-eight-year-old mother of one, with a child on the way, had been married only ten months. She was a customer in the credit union and had fallen three floors. She went into cardiac arrest in an ambulance and died.

Police and firefighters were helped in the search by other federal workers; Tony Lippe is an Oklahoma County Jail nurse who joined paramedics in searching the day-care center:

The 10:00 P.M. news on Monday, April 24, was showing a home video of two brothers who were killed in the bombing. I recognized the youngest brother as a little boy that I had tried to save and had carried out of the building. Now I knew the little boy's name was Colton Smith; he was two years old.

On Tuesday, April 25, Tony Lippe attended the funeral of Colton and Chase Smith. Their mother, Edye Smith, had heard him on a TV call-in the previous night and wanted to meet him. At the graveside they hugged.

Chance determined the fate of several people. A secretary called in late; someone else missed a turn and, because of traffic, missed the bomb. A lawyer was cursing at a stoplight when the blast blew his car into a wall; had the light been green, he almost

certainly would have been killed. Some people who would normally have been working in the Federal Building and were not, felt guilty about escaping when they saw what happened to colleagues. Some others who survived found afterward that strange premonitions had been stirred, like Richard Clough, who worked for the General Accounting Office on the third floor of the Murrah Building. He escaped with a broken leg, having dug himself out of the rubble:

After being treated by our family clinic, I called my mother. She told me that on the previous Saturday night she saw a vision or dream…a large building with black smoke rising from the top. She could not identify the building and had never seen my office. As she saw the building she began calling for me, but I never answered. Afterward she felt a strong urging to pray and did so that night and much of the time until very early Wednesday morning, the morning of the bombing. At that time she felt the urging to pray leave her. (The GAO office in the Federal Building was due to be closed in July 1995.)

By the end of the morning, it was obvious where the rescuers had had their most harrowing experiences: in the ruins of the day-care center. Fifteen children and three workers had died there. A lucky survivor was five-year-old Christopher Nguyen, the son of a Vietnamese family. He was addicted to Ninja Turtles and Power Rangers and was playing with water in the day-care center rest room when the bomb went off—giving him more protection than other children.

Some survivors, when they were rescued, desperately sought colleagues. One was Lorri McNiven, who worked in the Social Security office:

I was concerned about my fellow workers. I could not sit any longer, so I got up, barefoot, and started looking for the people I worked with. I was wandering around downtown Oklahoma City, soaking wet, shivering from the cold and shock, barefoot, practically blind, and totally overwhelmed. A lady came up and asked, "Is there anything I can do for you?" I asked her if she could take me home. She was my guardian angel that day. All I wanted was to get home, get into a shower, and get warm.

It was impossible for rescuers to know if people they brought out of the Federal Building with serious injuries had survived. Two police sergeants, Keith Simonds and Richard Williams, had rescued a woman early after the blast. Sergeant Simonds:
Sergeant Williams came from the basement soaking wet. He asked for my assistance, and we went into a completely black hole with only his flashlight to guide us over the rubble, the desks that were broken down, the doors that were blown off the hinges and blown in half, the concrete, and the wall partitions. The water was about six to seven inches deep and rising quickly. We made it to the woman, and Richard grabbed her by the legs and I grabbed her by the upper torso. While we were carrying her out, Richard got tied up in some electrical wires. We had to get him untangled. Once we made it to the sidewalk, I looked down at the victim and noticed that her right eye was swollen shut, and saw some tissue on her cheek. I saw that my right hand was in an open wound; I was holding on to her upper-arm bone.

I went with Richard the next day to a counseling debriefing, and we both thought that the woman had died. Richard started a search for her and was told that she was in intensive care at Presbyterian Hospital. She had been listed as Jane Doe for four days. Finally, she was identified as Falesha Bradley, the sister of Daina Bradley. [Daina Bradley was still trapped in the building; her story is on page 76.] She was alive! This was a moment that I will never forget.

The bomb separated husbands and wives. Germaine A. Johnson saw a tragic instance of this for a colleague at HUD on the seventh floor:
Bob Chumard and Larry Harris appeared in front of me. Bob's desk was on the west end of the floor, but his wife, Terry Rees, worked in public housing on the east end, just a few feet north of me. He came looking for her. He saw that all of the public housing area was gone. They both seemed to be calm and in control; they said they weren't leaving without me. I considered whether I should take my blue Loan Management 1992 coffee mug. It was still sitting there filled with sugar-free lemon candies. I decided against it. As Bob and I came onto the plaza, I looked up and saw Mike Reyes sitting on the ledge of the third or fourth floor. He had been on the seventh floor and had ridden a piece of the floor down. He had somehow been flipped onto the ledge instead of being crushed between the floors. He waved and said he was okay. Bob and I walked across Robinson, and Bob said, matter-of-factly, "I've lost my wife," and I answered, "Yes, Bob, she's gone." He actually went back and helped rescue others.

In Oklahoma City, the normal 911 traffic is around eighty calls an hour; during the first thirty minutes after the bombing, there were 338 calls. An incident command center had gone into action. Fire chief Gary Marrs and his deputy, Jon Hansen, were at the center of a system designed to handle natural disasters, not a bombing. Meanwhile, families with members working in the building now began trying to locate them, and hospitals found themselves handling not only casualties but also desperate relatives.

"DR. CHRISTOPHER, PHASE 4" That's code for catastrophe at St. Anthony Hospital, just one of the area hospitals put into instant overdrive. One woman, mistakenly informed that her grandson had been admitted here, said, "I don't know what to do other than go in there in a doctor's coat and start looking around."

ER: THE FIRST
Some victims even drove themselves

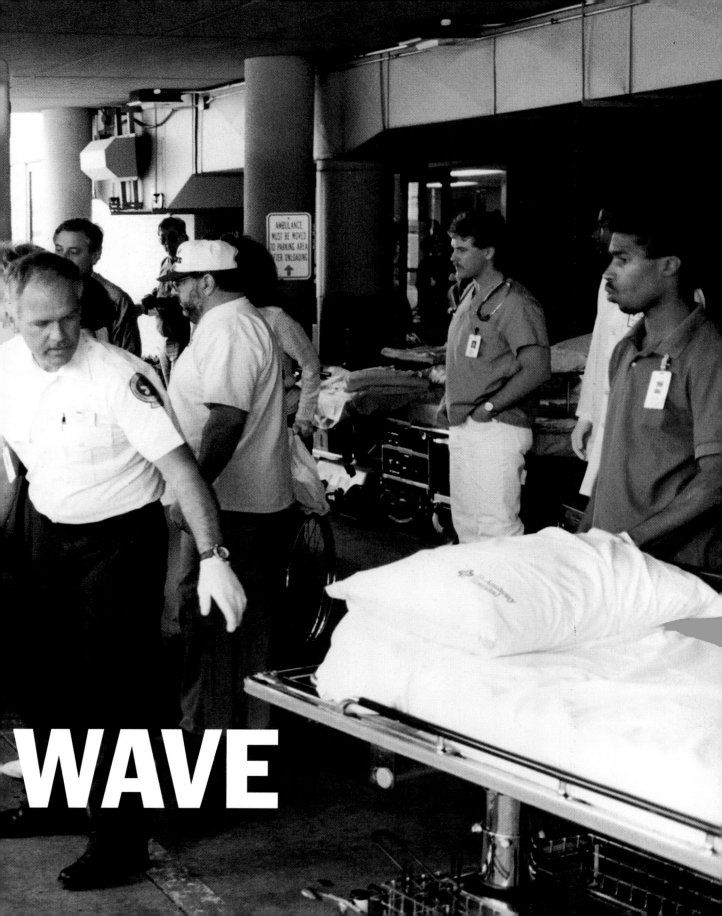

WAVE

The nearest hospital to the Federal Building, St. Anthony, was only eight blocks away. Within thirty minutes of the explosion the hospital had established a full trauma center with a team that included two ER physicians, orthopedic surgeons, neurosurgeons, and heart specialists. Many of the first sixty casualties ended up there, and there was a doctor ready for every one of them. The same was true at other hospitals: University, Children's, Baptist, and Presbyterian, which, among them, received the greatest number of injured. But although the response was practiced, the degree of the carnage shocked even veteran doctors. As the first wave of victims arrived in a makeshift fleet of ambulances, police cars, vans, some victims even driving themselves, more staff were called because a second, more serious, wave of injuries seemed inevitable once rescuers had worked through the building. By the end of the day, St. Anthony Hospital had treated 153 victims, Presbyterian more than 70, University 41, Children's 18. But a second wave never came.

Agnes "Pinky" Webster worked on the south side of the YMCA Building, with a clear view of the Federal Building:
The explosion shattered the windows, and the ceiling seemed to fall on me in slow motion. I heard the employees I supervised screaming. I moved from office to office checking to be sure everyone was out. I put my hand to my breast without looking down. I felt two pieces of glass protruding like knives out of stab wounds. I pulled them out and dropped them somewhere in the hall. I was the last person to leave the sixth floor. Outside the building I found Crystal, our executive secretary. Her head was bleeding and she was beginning to shake. I found my car and noticed it had a shattered windshield. I told Crys-

tal to get in, but she said, "No, I'll get blood all over your car." She would only sit in the door frame. A man walked over and gave her his jacket and urged Crystal to get in the car. We were told to drive to the hospital. Nina, another secretary, had joined us. I felt as if I were watching myself and the others in a movie. I couldn't see through my windshield. I have a very vivid memory of observing all the traffic lights and even using my turn signals. At the hospital, I saw the medical personnel waiting by the ER door as I attempted to turn into a parking space. I drove up on a curb, parked, and walked to the emergency-room door. I heard a voice say, "There's your patient right there." Two people put me in a wheelchair and took me in.

Thomas P. Janssen, Chief of Orthopedic Surgery at St. Anthony Hospital:
The injuries I saw were different from what I normally treated, with a preponderance of deep and superficial lacerations and eye injuries caused by flying glass. One patient, in military uniform, had received most of her injuries to the right side of the body. On the left side her shirt and pant leg were neatly pressed and clean. On the other side, her clothes were torn and tattered and bloodstained.

Melissa Craft is an oncology nurse at Presbyterian Hospital:
I was now in a MASH unit. I am a specialized, master's-prepared oncology nurse. I take care of cancer patients. But trauma? What do I know about trauma? I didn't begin to know what I could do for these bleeding, hurting people. A nurse who had been assisting with one patient asked me to help start another IV on him. I could see no veins to start an IV because there was blood all over his

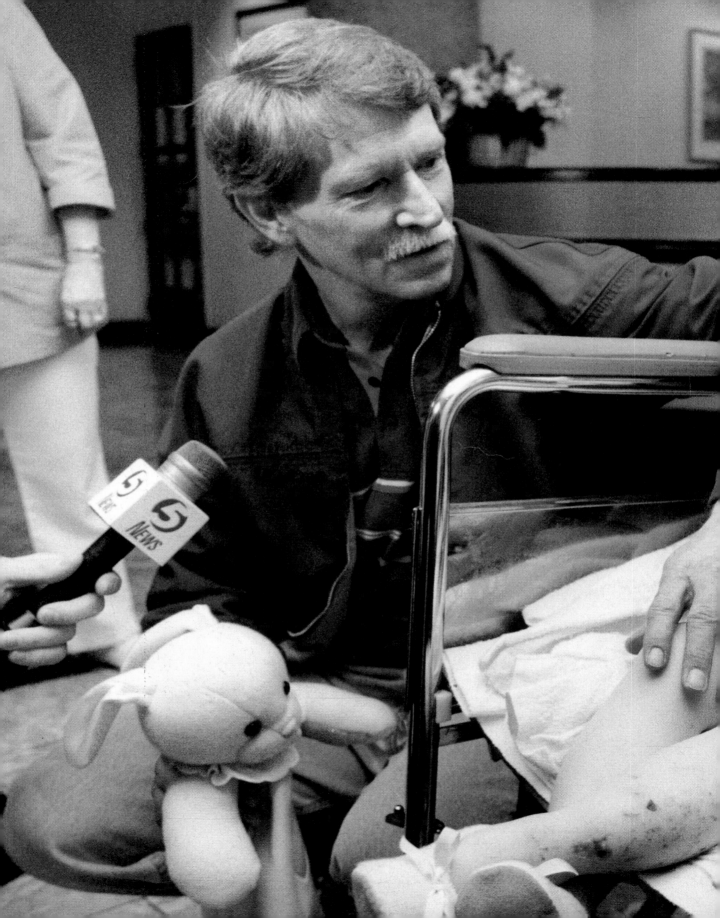

SMALL VICTORY
Rebecca Denny, two, left Southwest Medical Center on April 29; her brother Brandon, three, remained on the critical list. Despite the glass, cement, and plastic embedded in her left side, "Rebecca," said her father (left), "doesn't seem to be jittery or scared."

arm and hand. Then the doctor decided the first IV was fine. The victim's spinal X rays showed no injury to his spine, so we could take him off his back board. Other than that, and telling us his name was Fred and not Frank as it was written on his toe tag, he had not said much. We discovered a large laceration on his neck all the way to his carotid artery, where the glass was still embedded. It could potentially sever the artery. He would have to go to surgery, and we needed a cardio-vascular surgeon immediately. We simply yelled out what we needed and got it. Within minutes a superb cardiovascular surgeon was standing at his side. As I went into the operating room area, I real-ized I only had on "footies" and a mask—no hair cover and no scrubs. I began to question whether I should be in there like that until one of the OR nurses said "It's okay, we need all the help we can get!" The other nurse and I assisted with the trans-fer of Fred to the OR table, we told him goodbye, bagged his belongings, and left. I prayed for him. I realized then that in the midst of chaos and in my feelings of inadequacy, I had found a focus: I had become a trauma nurse for one patient when he needed me. I saw "my" patient two days after his surgery, sitting up in ICU with a large dressing on his neck. I asked him how he was, and he said, "Good, except my neck hurts." I laughed and said, "Believe me, your neck has a right to hurt!" My heart felt lighter.

Rita Cink is a registered nurse in the emergency room of Presbyterian Hospital.:
I was at the triage desk, and at 6:00 P.M. a young couple came in. The wife had sustained injuries. The man said, "My wife was in the bombing and we have been looking for our eighteen-month-old son all day." She looked so lifeless that I had to check her injuries before inquiring further about

BALLROOM, BLOODBANK
A function room at the Enlisted Club at Tinker Air Force Base suddenly serves as both. Here, civilians and military give blood and watch the news; outside this frame, over two hundred donors wait their turn.

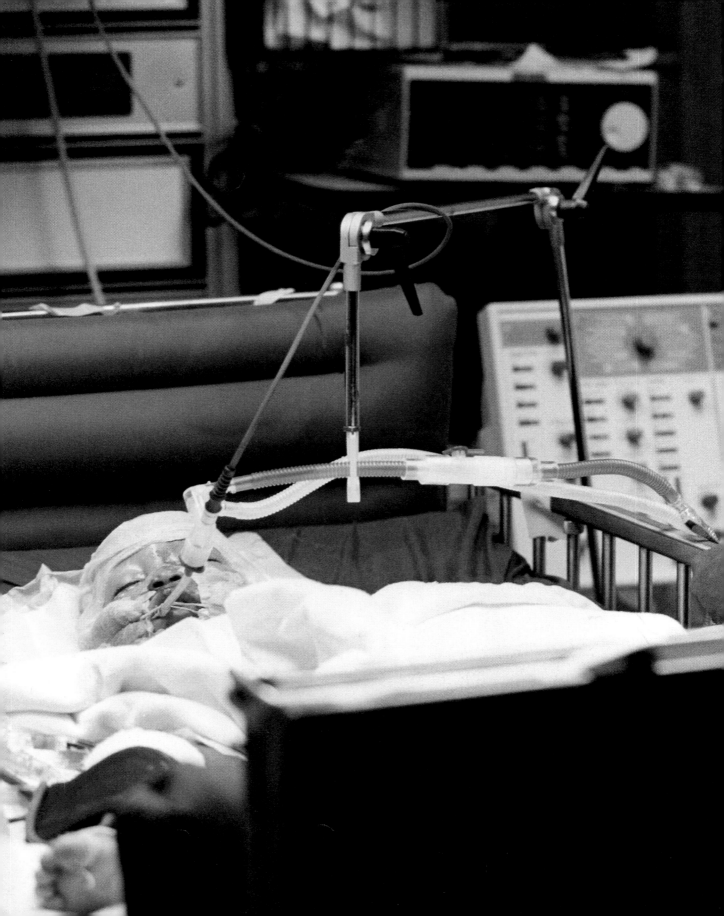

her son. Her face was swollen on the left side and was already blue. She had a laceration on her right knee and her left knee was bruised. She had been hit in the back and was having back pain. She did not appear emergent, so I called our supervisor to take the father to our auditorium, where victims were being identified. She would not let her husband leave, so the grandfather was contacted and sent to the auditorium. She was my last patient this shift. She had walked everywhere all day long, injured, looking for her baby. Her heart hurt worse than any injury she could have sustained. For me, it was the last straw for a very emotional day. You do your job with all the blood and bones, do it well, never look up, and then something like that makes you stop and brings you down.

The woman was Laura Kennedy. Her son, eighteen-month-old Blake Ryan, died.

The only serious casualty among the early volunteer rescuers was Rebecca Anderson, a nurse who went into the Federal Building to help look for survivors. Fred Anderson is her husband:

The hospital paged me and told me that my wife had been involved in the blast. I explained to them that we had gone down there to help and had become separated. They were confused about what had happened to her and could find no outer damage. The CAT scan of her brain showed light hemorrhaging in the frontal lobes and also from a blow in the back of the head. She went to surgery at 8:30 that night. She went up and down after that. They couldn't get the swelling under control. Basically, her brain swelled up and killed itself. Had she lived, it was unlikely that she could ever do nursing again. She wouldn't have liked that. Bec wouldn't have considered herself a hero. She was just doing her job in life.

INTO THE PIT

"It's great to see you, Daina. Hang on."

A grim coherence replaced the "organized chaos" of the hours immediately after the blast. It was now known what had happened. A massive bomb, a 4,800-pound cocktail of fertilizer and fuel oil, had been set off by a detonator in a Ryder rental truck parked at the main doors of the Murrah Building. The first wave of superhot gas moved at 7,000 miles an hour. Anyone ten feet away would be hit with a force equal to thirty-six tons. In about half a second, the gas dissipated and was replaced by an equally violent vacuum, sucking back debris that had been blown out. The shock wave from the bomb was powerful enough to tear up the inner structure of buildings many blocks away, as well as to pulverize windows in every direction.

Inside the gutted Murrah Building, the most dangerous area for the rescuers had already earned the name the pit. The full force of the bomb had blasted into the southeast corner of the building. Police sergeant Dan Helmuth was one of the first to stumble upon the consequences. He reported: "A cavelike area had been formed when a large slab of concrete from the floor above fell on two separate piles of rubble, ten to fifteen feet apart. More rubble had then fallen on top of the slab. At the cave opening, the roof was about five feet high. It then sloped downward to meet the lower floor, making the cave twenty to thirty feet deep." The

building was unstable (rainwater was feared as a potential factor in altering the weight and balance), and the pit was an extremely dangerous place to be. During the course of the day, the prolonged effort to free one victim who was trapped down there demanded great courage.

This story is told by police sergeant Kevin G. Thompson and Dr. Andy Sullivan, an orthopedic surgeon at Children's Hospital:

Sergeant Thompson: A fire captain almost up against the north wall said he had found another victim alive, a woman. He pointed to a large pile of concrete. I could now hear this lady talking to us. She was very calm and did not sound as if she was in pain. I bent down and looked but could only see a small part of her lower back. I looked at what was on top of her—tons and tons of concrete covered almost all of her. I felt absolutely useless, and I knew the fire captain felt the same. It was in his eyes and face. We had only our hands, no tools to work with, but the captain was on his radio asking for equipment. I noticed debris falling; as I looked up, I could see that about ten feet above us was a ten-by-twenty-foot slab of concrete hanging by only a couple of two-inch pieces of rebar. I knew that if it fell, we would die.

Dr. Sullivan: Only one person at a time could be in the space. We were told that if we felt any

movement at all, we were to immediately crawl out. It became obvious that the woman's right leg, trapped by concrete, was totally destroyed below the knee. If we attempted to move the materials on top of her, almost certainly further collapse would occur, crushing her to death. The only solution seemed to be to amputate. Her left leg was free, as were her left arm and upper chest. I crawled down and gained access to her by lying on top of her (later I found out that both of her lungs had been crushed and that in her right chest she had a collapsed lung with blood in the lung cavity.) I cut two strands of nylon rope and gradually made a tourniquet by working both of them under her right leg, digging through rubble with my hands to gain enough room. Suddenly, the firemen yelled that we had to evacuate.

FIRE: All companies, come outta the building. Right now! Everybody evacuate.

About ninety minutes after the blast, this alarm, that there was another bomb, terminated the search. Some rescuers, in the middle of extricating victims, at first refused to leave, but they were ordered to. Precious time was lost (the hiatus lasted for about forty-five minutes). What exactly happened is unclear. A policeman remembers a fireman grabbing his microphone and shouting, "There's another bomb in the building."

Sergeant Thompson: When we were told that we could go back, I went into the pit with my flashlight. I asked the woman her name, and she said, "Daina." I tried to crawl as close to her as I could. I was about two feet away, but a huge concrete beam was between us. As I lay there, I felt water dripping on me. I looked up with my flashlight and realized that the "water" was blood dripping from a crushed body above us. It was as if the concrete were bleeding. There was all this equipment beside me—jaws-of-life, power saws— and I didn't know to use it. I felt so useless. I looked back up the tunnel and saw a lone fireman and yelled up to him. He came down and said he knew how to use the equipment. As he lay there assessing the situation, blood dripped onto his yellow helmet until it became a red helmet. He backed out of the hole, saying, "It looks bad." I asked his name. He said it was Jeff. In the next two to three hours in that hole with him, I grew to respect Jeff as a true hero.

Later, when the firemen had removed enough debris for me to see Daina for the first time face-to-face, I said, "It's great to see you, Daina. Hang on. It won't be much longer."

Dr. Sullivan: The time outside was probably fortuitous: It allowed us to plan. Crawling back into the space, I realized the only way we could extract the patient was by a through-the-knee amputation. We had the firemen position a harness under her chest so that once the amputation was complete, we could pull her rapidly out onto a spine board. I discussed the choice with the patient. While tearful, she understood. I was fearful she might not survive much longer. She was already hypothermic, hypotensive, and having difficulty breathing.

Sergeant Thompson: A fresh crew of firemen came down and relieved Jeff, who had been working non-stop for several hours. A doctor asked me to go outside and bring him a trauma kit. I located a kit and started back down. I was stopped by a fire captain and he told me I couldn't go back. At first, I wanted to push my way down, but I realized he was just doing his job and I was tired and ready to get out.

Dr. Sullivan: Daina agreed to the surgery. I crawled back out. Dr. Stewart had selected a dose of Versed, and Dr. Tuggle crawled in and administered the anesthetic intramuscularly. Although we had some Demerol, we were afraid that it would suppress her respiration and stop her breathing. Versed had the advantage of being hypnotic and amnesic. Lying on top of Daina, I twisted the two nylon ropes with a stick to cut off remaining circulation to the leg. Using disposable blades and eventually an amputation knife, I was gradually able to work my way through the knee. Once the ligaments, tendons, and muscles had been cut, I cut through the remaining arteries, veins, and nerves at the back of the knee. The tourniquets worked so that she was not at risk of bleeding to death. We were then able to crawl out. The firemen were able to get on the harness and pull her out onto the spine board.

Sergeant Thompson: I wandered around for the next thirty minutes, looking at all the destruction. Later I spotted Jeff Hail, the fireman. He looked like a proud father. He said, "She's out, we did it, we helped get Daina out and she is going to live." It was now raining hard. I don't know why, but we hugged, and I felt like Jeff was the brother I never had. In some strange way we had bonded as if we had been lifelong friends.

That night, the rain added to the foreboding about a change in the task ahead. Instead of a search for survivors, it would become a drawn-out search for bodies. As yet, there was no accurate count of the missing. Worst estimates put the number in hundreds. By that evening, calls had gone out from Oklahoma City to teams of rescue specialists in other parts of the country. But as Daina Bradley was being treated in the hospital (she would recover well, but she had lost her two children and her mother), another person was found alive in the rubble. Initially, it was reported that there were four survivors at the base of the collapsed building, but in fact, there was only one, a young woman pressed between other bodies. The story is told by Bob Burton, a volunteer firefighter from Choctaw, Oklahoma:

At about 7:00 P.M., as Allen Adkisson and I entered the collapsed area, we asked everyone to be quiet. Someone thought he had heard a moan. Allen and I screamed in the quiet night asking if anyone could hear us. It was then I heard a muffled cry for help. I isolated the cry and found a young woman buried. Jerry McKee worked his way to her feet, where he uncovered a tennis shoe. Allen, Theda Adkisson, and I removed debris and talked to her, reassuring her that help was on the way. I asked her what her name was, and she said, "Brandi." I said I had a niece named Brandi. She told me she was fifteen and that she had asthma and a heart murmur. Eventually, I freed her hand and she grasped mine and would not let go.

An hour and a half passed, and Dr. Rick Nelson showed up from above. He moved debris and cut plumbing to help us gain better access. He quickly became part of our team. The storm approached and debris fell on us. I was lying sandwiched between rebar and concrete and, looking up for the first time, I noticed huge chunks of concrete dangling from rebar. I thought, "This is not a safe situation." If anything shifted in the structure at this point, I would be crushed or pinned along with the other members of this team. The area was very unstable and isolated. Fire personnel showed up with a shoring team to relieve us and complete extrication. I told Brandi we would see her again soon, on the outside, but it was very difficult to transfer her clenching hand to her new caretaker, Dr. Nelson.

Brandi Liggons was the last survivor.

OPEN TO THE SKY
Lacking a steel frame, the Murrah Building
relied for strength on reinforced concrete,
which disintegrated in the blast. The transfer
beam, top right, was completely severed,
exposing rebar. Rescue teams were surprised
by the amount of powdered concrete—
survivors were often coated in it

A PROFILE OF LETHAL FORCE
Around the site, an army of experts

The bomb came very close to blowing away the whole Federal Building. From the air, the scalloped profile of the roof reveals with chilling precision how and where the blast penetrated the structure. The southern wall and elevator shaft help hold together what remains. As the graphics on the following pages show, what little stability the building retained was also perilously dependent on a few reinforced-concrete pillars. Many of the rescuers reported debris that was thick with rebar—the steel reinforcement used inside concrete. The deepest penetration of the blast was at the eastern end, where there is no staircase left inside the wall. In the days following the blast, a small army of experts directed the search at the site. Some of their resources are visible in the photograph: the temporary morgue, which played a key role in identifying victims as they were found, and tents where evidence was sifted for the investigation into the bombing, which had to run concurrently with the search for victims (the FBI sifted debris at the site and, again, when it was removed to another location). Some of the extensive damage to other buildings is visible, as are the scorch marks on roofs where burning pieces of cars were hurled.

The Pit   The Pancake   Robinson Avenue

First Methodist Church, dating from 1890s (stained glass windows blown out)

Temporary Morgue for Victim IDs

Refrigerated Trucks for Bodies

Fifth Street YMCA (severely damaged, including day-care center)

ATF/FBI Evidence Tents

Crater Site

Parking Lot (cars burned, gas tanks and tires exploded, main source of smoke)

Journal Record Building (severe internal and external damage and many people seriously injured)

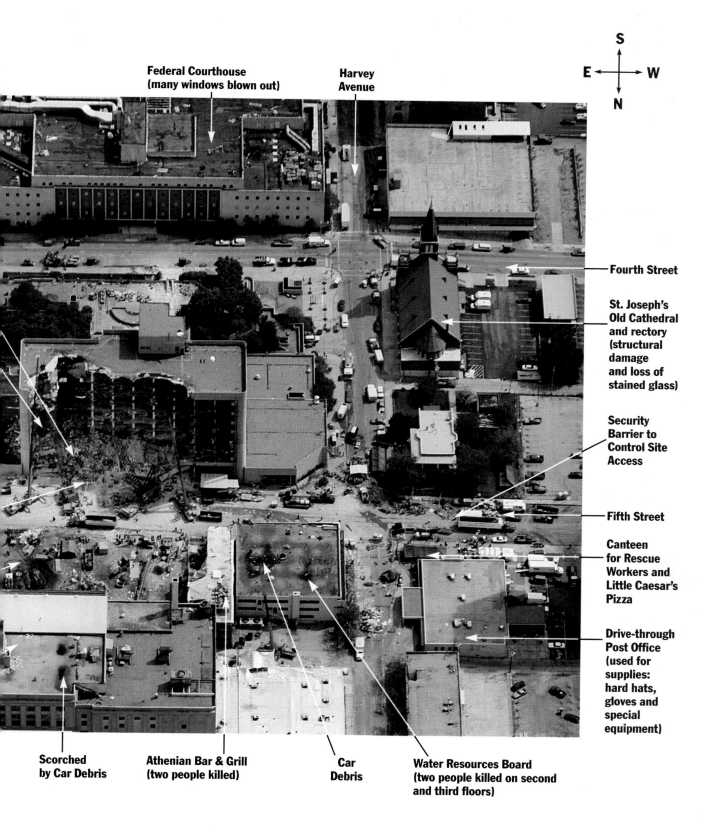

S
E ← → W
N

Federal Courthouse (many windows blown out)

Harvey Avenue

Fourth Street

St. Joseph's Old Cathedral and rectory (structural damage and loss of stained glass)

Security Barrier to Control Site Access

Fifth Street

Canteen for Rescue Workers and Little Caesar's Pizza

Drive-through Post Office (used for supplies: hard hats, gloves and special equipment)

Scorched by Car Debris

Athenian Bar & Grill (two people killed)

Car Debris

Water Resources Board (two people killed on second and third floors)

83

Within seconds, the bomb rearranged the physical nature of the Federal Building as it forcibly redistributed people who were in it. The combination of these two things—structural deformation and scores of bodies to be located—created a technical challenge that few people understood. One who did was a stocky, silver-haired fire chief from New York City called Ray Downey. Early in the afternoon of April 19, Downey was called by FEMA and asked to get to Oklahoma City as soon as he could. Downey is an urban search-and-rescue specialist; he was called in after the World Trade Center bombing, and he had an esoteric skill that was critically needed in Oklahoma City: He could "read the wreck."

Specialists like Downey, usually drawn from fire departments, develop an instinct after years of dealing with buildings in various states of destruction. They can look at a wreck and instantly know all the danger signs. They can, for example, see what they call "widow-makers"—debris left hanging that can fall and kill. They also have a graphic term for people who fall several or many floors in a collapse: "taking the slide."

When Ray Downey first looked at the Federal Building on the night of April 19, he could tell that many people had taken the slide. In fact, plotting just who had ended up where would be, over the coming days, one of his most agonizing tasks. When Downey "read a wreck," he established the exact physical whereabouts of victims at the time of the explosion. Anecdotal details mattered. He looked out for "creatures of habit," someone who would have been at a coffee machine, for example. He wanted to know the color of carpet, the color of wall paint, the seating plan in a conference room.

Armed with these details, he would then look at the way the building collapsed and project where within the debris he would most likely find the clues

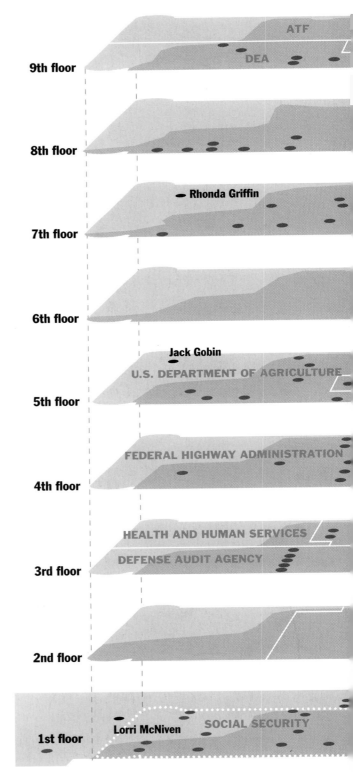

WHERE THEY WERE

ATF
DEA
9th floor

8th floor

Rhonda Griffin
7th floor

6th floor

Jack Gobin
U.S. DEPARTMENT OF AGRICULTURE
5th floor

FEDERAL HIGHWAY ADMINISTRATION
4th floor

HEALTH AND HUMAN SERVICES
DEFENSE AUDIT AGENCY
3rd floor

2nd floor

SOCIAL SECURITY
Lorri McNiven
1st floor

MEETING ROOM

SECRET SERVICE

DEA

HUD

Sandy Teel

Robyn Parent

DEA

HUD

VACANT

USMC RECRUITING

STORE ROOM

VETERANS ADMINISTRATION

HUD

U.S. CUSTOMS

Stan Rombaun

John Colvin

Raymond Washburn

SNACK BAR

ARMY RECRUITING

Clark C. Peterson

Nancy Ingram

Steve Pruitt

GENERAL ACCOUNTING

Richard Clough

FEDERAL EMPLOYEES CREDIT UNION

ARMY

(Exact locations unknown)

DAY CARE

GSA

● Fatalities   ● Survivors who tell their stories in the text   ▭ Area destroyed by blast

WORKING THE BELLY OF THE BEAST

Timeline of events

Day 1

9:05 A.M.
Police and firefighters begin to arrive. Scores of untrained individuals are swarming in and out of the wrecked building in an attempt to help.

About 10:30 A.M.
A bomb scare does what the rescue professionals cannot – it clears the building.

7:00 P.M.
Brandi Liggons, fifteen, is found alive and freed hours later – the last survivor.

Day 2

1:00 A.M.
The first out-of-state search-and-rescue team starts work at the site.

The upper floors are thoroughly searched, but no one is found alive. Reshoring the building is a priority.

Days 3-5

Debris removal is slow-going. Cranes must lift the massive pieces of shattered concrete gingerly to avoid crushing any victims.

Days 6-7

Rubble is carried out at a rate of 100 tons a day.

Days 8-10

Peak of work; with the aid of a 100-ton crane, rubble is removed at a rate of 350 tons a day.

Day 16

The declining area of work space reduces the need for workers. By the time operation ends, only about fifteen "rubble-surfers" are still digging.

Rescuers know that victims remain buried at the base of Column 22, but as they attempt to remove them, the column shifts ominously. On May 4, at 11:50 P.M., Oklahoma City special operations chief Mike Shannon states, "I'm calling the game."

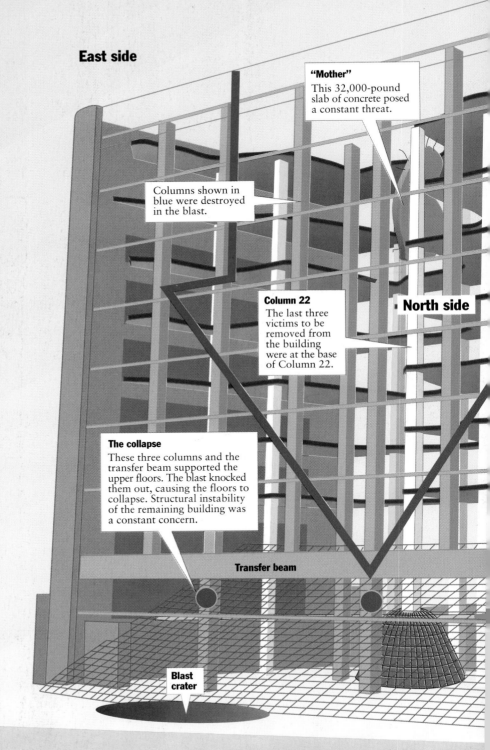

East side

"Mother"
This 32,000-pound slab of concrete posed a constant threat.

Columns shown in blue were destroyed in the blast.

Column 22
The last three victims to be removed from the building were at the base of Column 22.

North side

The collapse
These three columns and the transfer beam supported the upper floors. The blast knocked them out, causing the floors to collapse. Structural instability of the remaining building was a constant concern.

Transfer beam

Blast crater

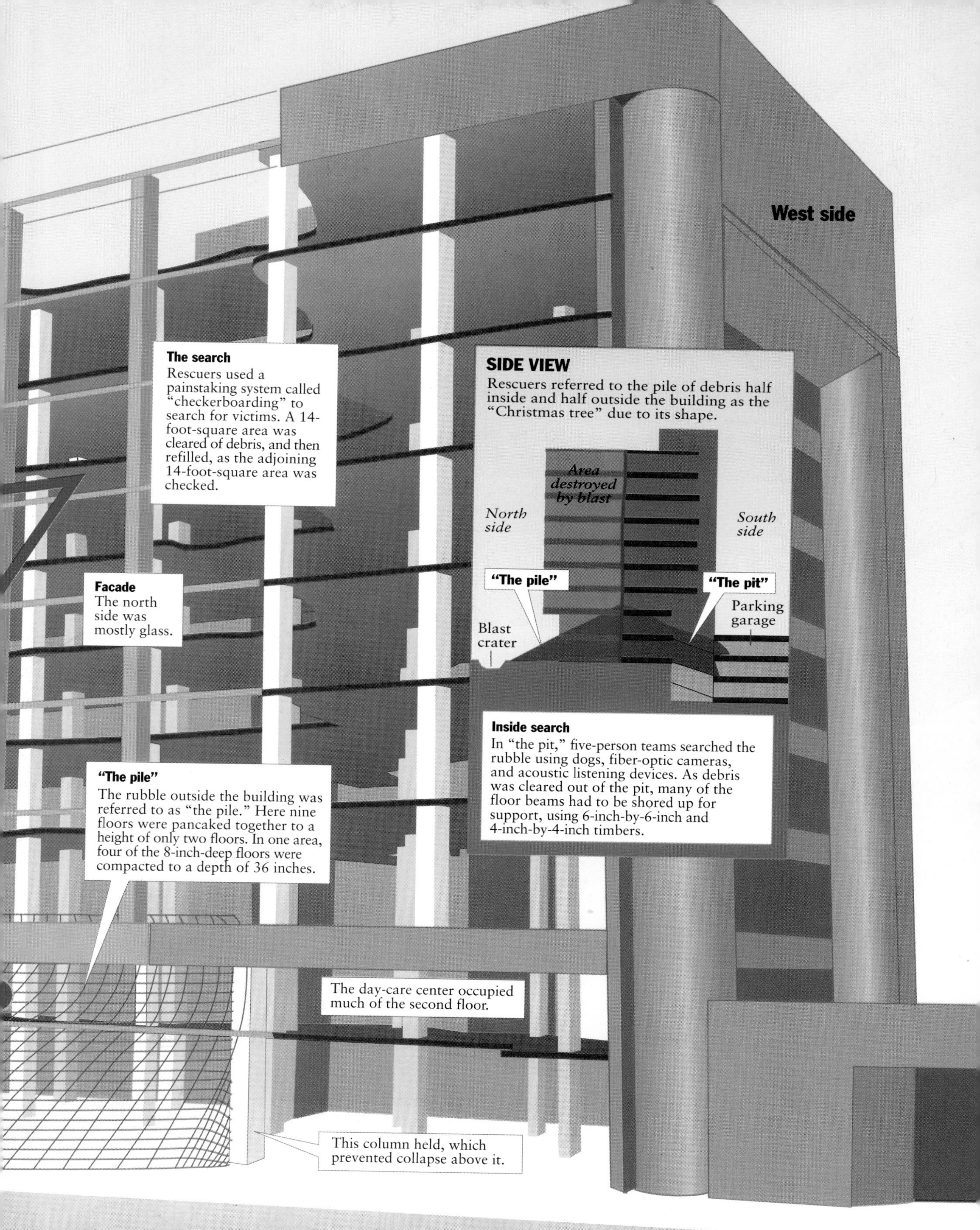

West side

The search
Rescuers used a painstaking system called "checkerboarding" to search for victims. A 14-foot-square area was cleared of debris, and then refilled, as the adjoining 14-foot-square area was checked.

SIDE VIEW
Rescuers referred to the pile of debris half inside and half outside the building as the "Christmas tree" due to its shape.

Area destroyed by blast

North side

South side

"The pile"

"The pit"

Parking garage

Blast crater

Facade
The north side was mostly glass.

Inside search
In "the pit," five-person teams searched the rubble using dogs, fiber-optic cameras, and acoustic listening devices. As debris was cleared out of the pit, many of the floor beams had to be shored up for support, using 6-inch-by-6-inch and 4-inch-by-4-inch timbers.

"The pile"
The rubble outside the building was referred to as "the pile." Here nine floors were pancaked together to a height of only two floors. In one area, four of the 8-inch-deep floors were compacted to a depth of 36 inches.

The day-care center occupied much of the second floor.

This column held, which prevented collapse above it.

ANSWERING THE CALL

FEMA, the Federal Emergency
Management Agency,
sent ten teams to Oklahoma City.
Experienced in natural disasters,
they had to adapt to America's
worst terrorist bombing.

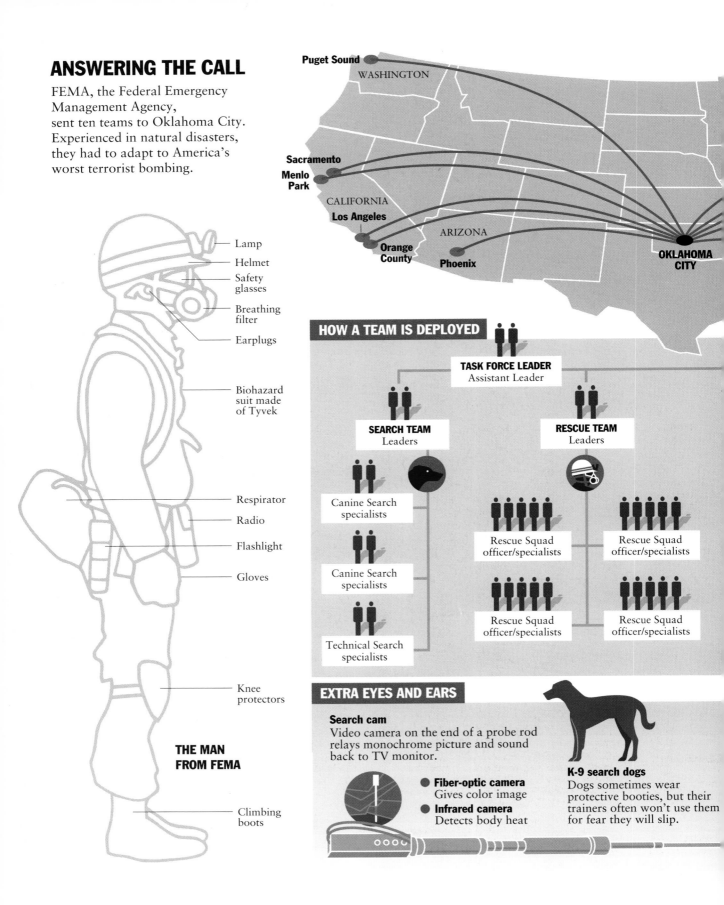

Puget Sound
WASHINGTON

Sacramento
Menlo
Park

CALIFORNIA
Los Angeles
Orange
County

ARIZONA

Phoenix

OKLAHOMA
CITY

THE MAN FROM FEMA

- Lamp
- Helmet
- Safety glasses
- Breathing filter
- Earplugs
- Biohazard suit made of Tyvek
- Respirator
- Radio
- Flashlight
- Gloves
- Knee protectors
- Climbing boots

HOW A TEAM IS DEPLOYED

TASK FORCE LEADER
Assistant Leader

SEARCH TEAM
Leaders

RESCUE TEAM
Leaders

Canine Search specialists

Canine Search specialists

Technical Search specialists

Rescue Squad officer/specialists

Rescue Squad officer/specialists

Rescue Squad officer/specialists

Rescue Squad officer/specialists

EXTRA EYES AND EARS

Search cam
Video camera on the end of a probe rod
relays monochrome picture and sound
back to TV monitor.

● **Fiber-optic camera**
Gives color image

● **Infrared camera**
Detects body heat

K-9 search dogs
Dogs sometimes wear
protective booties, but their
trainers often won't use them
for fear they will slip.

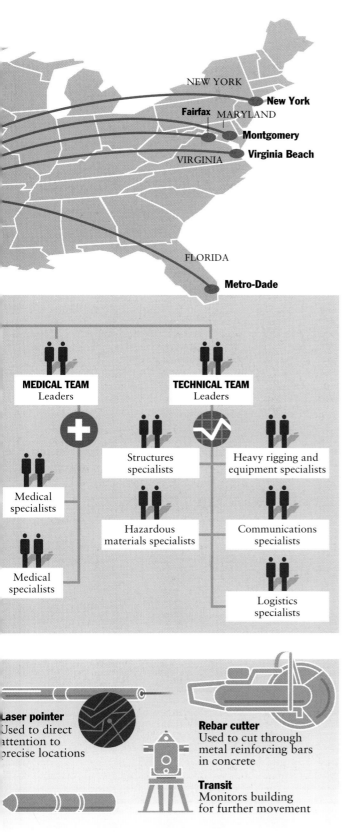

NEW YORK

New York

Fairfax MARYLAND

Montgomery

VIRGINIA

Virginia Beach

FLORIDA

Metro-Dade

MEDICAL TEAM
Leaders

TECHNICAL TEAM
Leaders

Structures specialists

Heavy rigging and equipment specialists

Medical specialists

Hazardous materials specialists

Communications specialists

Medical specialists

Logistics specialists

Laser pointer
Used to direct attention to precise locations

Rebar cutter
Used to cut through metal reinforcing bars in concrete

Transit
Monitors building for further movement

---

that would lead to the body: the carpet, the desk, the lamp. As he looked at the Federal Building, Downey saw great dangers. It was what he called, in his laconic way, "a dynamic situation." Meaning, nothing was stable. The first priority was to "blitz" the building with carefully directed rescuers to find anyone still alive. One characteristic of a collapsed building that rescuers always look for had already been identified before Downey arrived in Oklahoma City—the "voids," spaces formed within the falling debris in which people could survive for a limited time. The pit was one. Tragically, it turned out that the last survivor to be found alive, Brandi Liggons, was on her way to the hospital before Downey had his team in place.

As he appraised the building, overnight and then after dawn, Downey began to give expressive names, like "Mother," to areas of the wreck that would prove hazardous and intractable. At the site, Chief Downey was designated FEMA operations chief, working with Chief Mike Shannon of the Oklahoma Fire Department, who was in overall command of the search-and-rescue for the fire department.

Chief Downey:

My first impression was that the destruction was similar in amount to the destruction at the World Trade Center. Later, I determined that the Federal Building had significantly more damage to important components and was in much greater danger of further collapse. Chief Shannon knew the building's floor plans, stairways, elevators, and other data. Initially, we directed our efforts at any viable opening into which we could get search dogs, rescuers, search cams (video cameras on the end of probe rods that relay pictures back to TV monitors). Later, a bigger picture revealed many areas that would require dedicated rescue teams for the search. The pile, for example, was the remaining debris from the explosion and building collapse. Some referred to this section as the bowl, because of its shape. The south side was the remaining intact wall of the building. The east side had the remaining wall and portions of all nine floors that could only be accessed by ladder or the man-basket lifted by the crane. Where the pile was actually inside the building was the pit, in the southeast corner. Many of the beams and floors had to be shored up for support; this shoring came to be known as the forest (the demolition company that later imploded the building said that extra explosives were needed because of the quality of shoring).

At the beginning we had approximately 250 rescuers working twenty-four hours a day. As the size of the search area decreased, the need for rescuers decreased. We used K-9 search dogs, the search cams, seismic/acoustic listening devices and building transits, cross-hair monitors to measure movement in the structure (when the sun came out, the east wall would expand as much as half an inch). Transits also monitored "Mother," the fifteen-feet-by-thirty-feet concrete slab hanging from the ninth and eighth floors directly over the pile. "Mother" was a serious threat to the safety of all rescuers during the entire operation. We also had to contend with lightning, heavy rains, strong winds, bomb scares, building movement concerns, reported sightings of victim movement on upper floors, and even a psychic envisioning three victims awakening from unconsciousness and being trapped on the second floor. The rescuers never gave up hope of finding someone alive; the frustration of not finding anyone was overcome by the fact that the professional rescuers performed what would be one of the most difficult search-and-rescue operations without any loss of life or serious injury.

Police lieutenant John Clark arrived at the site just before 1:00 P.M. and worked until late that night:
I could not sleep. I wanted to tell the world how I felt. I went outside to my scout car and wrote "We Will Never Forget" on the back window with white shoe polish. I tied different-colored ribbons to my antennas. It seemed to make me feel better. Those four words meant a lot to me: that I would never forget the loss of life, the acts of mercy, the love, the unity, the hope, the rescue, the volunteers, the courage, the tears, and the prayers. The next day as I drove to the site, many people commented on the window. Soon, many officers wrote the same thing on their cars. It became a universal message.

David A. Grissam is with the Oklahoma County Sheriff's Office:
Early Thursday morning the entire team was asleep—all except incident commander Mike Jack. A strange feeling had come over him while he was lying on the garage floor at the west end of the Federal Building thinking how proud he was of the team. From out of nowhere came a lady. She covered him with a blanket. He said, "I asked her who she was, and she told me that she was a nurse and was here to help. She looked like an angel to me."

James L. Parker is a deputy U.S. marshal assigned to Salt Lake City. He was a member of the stress debriefing team. On April 27, he was trying to locate the body of Kathy, the wife of another U.S. marshal:
The pit was becoming more dangerous with time. I was amazed that anyone would even go in there, let alone work in it. As you looked up at the wall of cement and metal, you could see hands, feet, legs, and body parts. Then disaster almost hit us. Two large cement sections of flooring started to shift. None of the workers noticed. We started

EXHAUSTIVE SEARCH
"We're having a real hard time getting them to take a break," said one rescue team leader of workers who, despite grueling twelve-hour shifts in the shaky structure, hated the thought of slowing down.

DAMAGE CONTROL
Workers install steel bracing to prevent the Murrah Building from further collapse. Directly below the steel braces is the area known as the pit, still overlaid with tons of rubble. Much of this rubble was removed by hand, in five-gallon buckets.

yelling but were not being heard. Some of us realized that our masks were not allowing the screams to be heard. Ripping mine off, I have never yelled so loud in my whole life. The workers finally reacted. One man came so close to being crushed—I'm not sure how he made it. The next day we went back. The team came out with the body of Kathy, the lady we felt we had come to know. The flag was draped over her and the gurney was wheeled to a stop. As we all exited, there stood a large number of military, OCPD, and ATF agents at attention, saluting the flag and the lady under it. They didn't know who it was. They didn't have to. All they knew was that whoever was under that flag meant something to the U.S. Marshals Service. And she did.

Clayton D. Hoskinson is an investigator for the Oklahoma Department of Human Services:
I was directing traffic at Ninth and Harvey. This intersection was as close as pedestrians and traffic could get to the building. By mid-morning a fine mist had become a driving rain. I was cold, wet, and feeling miserable when a car, barely running, looking like it was held together with prayers and twine, pulled into the intersection. The driver cracked the window, allowing me to see only his eyes.

"Is this where I'm supposed to drop off the boots?" he asked. I had no information about a need for boots. The man said that he had just heard a plea on the radio for steel-toed boots. I told him that we could put the boots with other items, and he rolled down his window and handed me the boots. In the car with him were a woman, an infant, and two small children. Taking the boots, I immediately noticed they felt warm on the inside. Looking back into the car, I saw the man was wearing no shoes.

"Are these your boots?" I asked.

"Yes." He nodded.

"Sir, no one expects you to give up your own boots," I said as I attempted to hand them back through the window.

With a tear in his eye, he said, "There are people in there who need them worse than I do."

Barry K. Shisler is a member of the Air Force Reserve Fire Department at Tinker Air Force Base, Oklahoma. He was involved in the operation of the decontamination unit:
On the morning of May 5, I had just finished my last shift at the site. Early in the rescue operation, someone had spray-painted the words "BLESS THE CHILDREN + THE INNOCENT" on a jagged piece of concrete. Now, a maintenance truck arrived, loaded with toys, flowers, sympathy cards, and notes of thanks, all left by Oklahomans at street corners near the site as a tribute to victims, volunteers, and rescue workers. The truck crew and I decided to add the items to the concrete memorial. While we were working, a lovely volunteer handed me a white teddy bear. Attached to the bear was a blue-ribbon sash that read, "Thank you for your efforts." There was also a picture of an infant girl and a card that read, "In loving memory of Danielle Nicole Bell." The volunteer told me that the child was one of those in the daycare center and that the items came from a relative who wished them to be placed where the rescue workers could see them during the memorial service. It became a symbol for us of all those innocent souls we had hoped to save.

Brenda McDaniel worked in a canteen for the Salvation Army:
Early in the evening, an Oklahoma City third grade class had left a large box of paper sacks filled with candy and a decorated letter of thanks to the

rescue workers. During the night, an exhausted fireman came up, shaking, and asked for a cup of hot coffee. He had helped recover a victim and said he was having a hard time emotionally. I noticed he had one of the paper sacks in his hand. He said, "I'll be okay in a minute. I'm having flashbacks to Vietnam. You see, I was wounded in Nam, and while I lay waiting for someone to find me, a plane flew overhead and dropped little paper sacks and I had one close to me from a little girl in Pennsylvania. She was in the third grade, I still have it. Much later, I wrote to tell her how her letter had kept me alive. I can't believe it, here I am tonight with another letter from a third grader—just when I needed it." I poured him a cup of coffee, and he slipped away and asked for a chaplain. The two worked through the cruelty of this situation. It was clear that the experience helped the fireman. It helped me, too.

Sergeant Ronnie E. Burks is a member of the police department's K-9 (search dog) unit. After helping with the rescue of Daina Bradley, Sergeant Burks worked twelve-hour night shifts with his dog, Arlo. On the final night search, May 1, he worked with Sergeant Don Browning and his dog, Gunny. They were trying to locate any remaining victims: Almost everyone had left. Our dogs began indicating in the same areas. We would mark the spot with orange spray paint. The dogs were confirming each other's finds. During the initial rescue operations, the FEMA dogs had problems with being depressed and stressed out. Don and I came to the conclusion that the handlers became

depressed and this went right down the leash to the K-9. Both Arlo and Gunny appeared to boost each other's drive by working as a team. Both of them were accustomed to stress—nothing is more stressful than K-9 police work. When it became too dark to work, we marked six spots where we believed there were victims. I heard someone say, "Thank you," and, "God bless you." I turned around, and there was Mrs. Keating standing there just behind the tape. The First Lady gave us a boost of pride and energy to keep on working.

Later, firefighters recovered victims from all the hot spots we had marked.

Steven C. Davis is a corporal with the Oklahoma City Fire Department: While I was digging through a tangle of cement, steel, and broken wires, I ripped my boot on something sharp. I was issued a new pair of boots and, putting them on, found a scribbled note inside one boot. "God bless the man who wears these boots, that he may be strong in his search for life." I needed those words then. My wife, Tami, framed that note, and every time I look at it, I think, "God bless you too, my friend."

Disaster experts had predicted that, with the nature of the injuries sustained in the blast, no more than eighty percent of the victims would be identified. In fact, all were. This was a feat of science and dedication conducted under extremely stressful conditions. Remains were taken first to a temporary morgue at the site. Twenty-four people worked in this morgue, including sixteen special-

ists from the U.S. Army. Fingerprints, dental charts, and full-body X rays were used in identifying bodies, and DNA testing proved crucial in some of the most difficult cases (as it had, for example, in identifying victims of the Pan Am 103 disaster). The more sophisticated medical work was carried out in the State Medical Examiner's Office on the campus of the University of Oklahoma Health Sciences Center, where one hundred people were eventually involved. It so happened that Dr. Clyde Snow, one of the world's most acclaimed forensic anthropologists, was a faculty member at the university. Snow had worked for two decades with the Federal Aviation Administration to help identify the victims of air crashes; notably, he had also unearthed, in Bolivia, remains believed to be those of Butch Cassidy and the Sundance Kid.

Kevin Rowland is chief investigator for the Chief Medical Examiner's Office:

When I went to work on April 19, I took my lunch as I did on many days. I don't know whatever happened to it, but I never missed it. My responsibilities were helping set up the medical examiner's operations both at the morgue and at the scene. After the first day, I was responsible for the scene only. When I realized the second day that I only had two pairs of jeans and one pair of tennis shoes and no work boots, I knew I was in trouble.

I asked a man I had just met, Les Cummins, if he could get someone to run an errand for me. Les was with the Red Cross/FEMA logistics supplier for the temporary morgue site. I had never

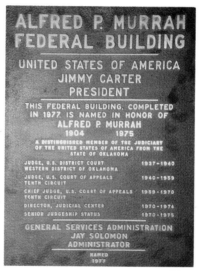

known Les or any of his people prior to this. He quickly said that whatever I needed, he would be happy to help. I tried to give him my credit card to go buy me some jeans and boots at Anthony's clothing store. Les refused my card and told me that what I needed would be taken care of. I didn't understand how this would be done, but I told him okay. About an hour later, I had several pairs of new jeans and a new pair of work boots. This was the first of many things that I would need over the eighteen days I was on the scene, and every need was met.

April 24 was my wife's birthday, and I again asked Les to take my credit card and get me a dozen roses for her birthday, since I had arranged to have her come to the scene so I could at least spend an hour or so with her. He again refused my card, and within an hour his wife showed up with a dozen yellow roses (my wife's favorite). These were donated by a florist.

I noticed when I was looking for my credit card that I didn't have any cash in my wallet. I checked my pocket and noticed that I was carrying fifty-five cents. When I left the scene on May 8, I had the same fifty-five cents in my pocket as the day I arrived on the scene. Even when I would stop on my way home for something, nobody would let me pay for anything. I was always told, "Sir, it's an honor to have served you." I would get teary-eyed every time this happened. I can assure you that Oklahomans are the greatest people in the world. I was told by a group of FBI agents that they voted to sell Washington, D.C., and move the nation's capital to Oklahoma.

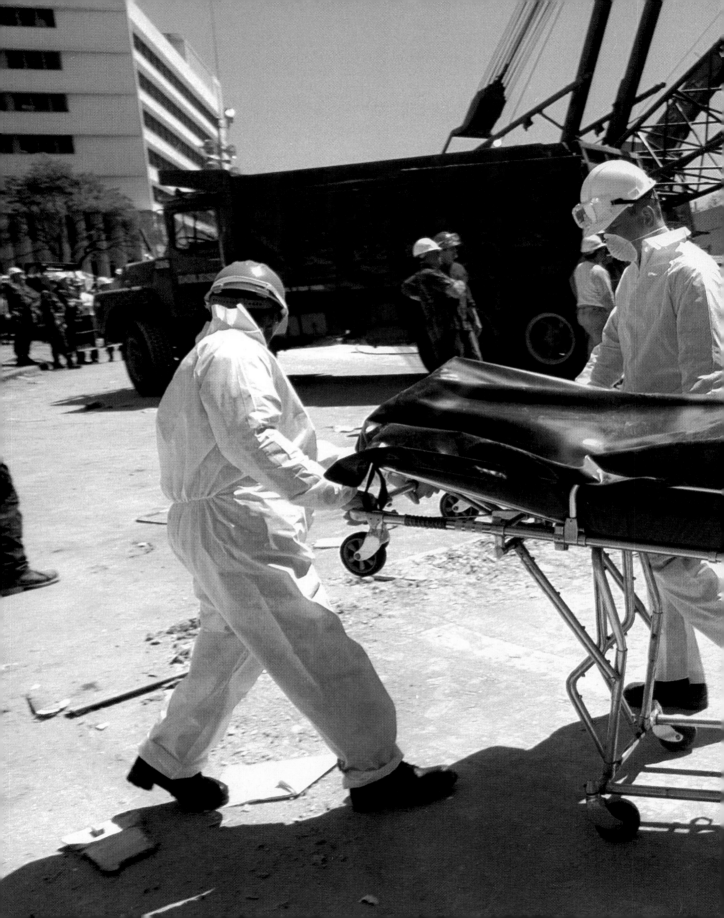

"HELP YOURSELF TO ANYTHING"
So read the sign in the garage of
the Southwestern Bell
Headquarters, the instant bazaar
and pharmacy where rescue
workers got twenty-four-hour
support. There were also masseurs
and barbers on hand.

Night operations in the Federal Building ended on May 1. In the floodlights, the ruptured concrete cage was starker than in daylight. The small improvised shrines to the children who died resembled cairns—piles of concrete shards topped with wreaths. At the top of the surviving, bare eastern wall, against a stellar heartland night sky, the Stars and Stripes flew, suspended from an improvised flagpole. By now, the original cascade of debris that had formed something like a steep glacier from the ninth floor to street level had been reduced to a dense core, the final tomb. By May 4, when the search effort concluded, the workers had removed 450 tons of debris, much of it by hand, carried in buckets to Dumpsters—every piece sifted for evidence of remains. At that time it was thought that two bodies remained in the core, which could not be further reduced without endangering the entire building. They were the bodies of Christy Rosas, twenty-two, who had worked in the third-floor credit union for only nine days, and Virginia Thompson, fifty-six, who had worked there for only eighty-nine days. Later, it turned out that a customer, fifty-four-year-old Alvin Justes, was also entombed. The core was painted a bright rust-orange so that when the building was finally brought down by a carefully planned implosion, the location of the bodies would be clear.

James L. Witt is the director of the Federal Emergency Management Agency (FEMA).

I never thought I would see an interagency partnership as united as it was in Oklahoma City, from Governor Keating to the mayor, local police chief, and local fire chief. It was just remarkable. We had search-and-rescue teams from the East Coast and the West Coast there to help. Our rescue workers told us they had never experienced the kind of love and support that was shown to them in Oklahoma City.

Sometimes, it took weeks for the truth to emerge about some of the victims in the Federal Building. The most extraordinary example of this is the case of Michael Loudenslager, who worked in the GSA offices in the northwest corner of the Federal Building—a small area slightly outside the main force of the blast. At 8:40 A.M. on Wednesday, he phoned his wife, Bettie, and said he was clearing his desk to get ready for a planned four-day weekend. There was no trace of Loudenslager in the forty-eight hours immediately after the bombing. Then, on Friday, April 21, his family was called to Presbyterian Hospital. There, a GSA colleague, with bad facial scars and numerous internal injuries, told the family that he had been pulled from the rubble by Michael Loudenslager, who appeared himself to be unhurt. The family still hoped he would be found alive. A day later, another GSA colleague attested that he, too, had been saved by Loudenslager. Apparently, Loudenslager had then headed for the second-floor day-care center (the center was part of the GSA, and GSA staffers often played with the children). After that, there was no sighting of him. Then, late on the night of Saturday, April 22, rescue workers found his body near the stairwell, under a vast concrete block. It took two shifts of men working with jackhammers to free him, and on Sunday morning, the day of the prayer service, Michael Loudenslager's family was formally notified of his death. It was then clear that he was the second fatality among people who tried to rescue victims. Rebecca Anderson, who died after being hit by concrete soon after the blast, had gone into the building from the street. Michael Loudenslager never made it to the street. His priority was the day-care center.

CLOSE COMPANIONS
Twenty-four man-and-dog teams, including Skip Fernandez and Aspen, from Miami, aided the rescue effort. "When [my dog] finds someone alive, he barks," said a worker. "When he finds a body, he whines...He's done more whining than barking."

A TRIBUTE BY TOM BROKAW

"For all of the work at hand, for all of the grief and anxiety,
Oklahoma City didn't set aside its manners: heroes showed up on time"

As a son of the Great Plains, I knew instinctively the response of the people of Oklahoma to the sudden, savage bombing of the crowded Federal Building in the heart of their capital, a community where working-class ethics, big money, and old-fashioned religious values are stitched together seamlessly.

First, the shock, for this is a place insulated by geography and a trusting innocence. Droughts, tornadoes, prairie fires, yes, but terrorist bombing? Here? The shock and bewilderment gave way instantly to the work to be done. In a state where lives are defined by real hands-on work, it was still astonishing to see how swiftly the job of rescuing the survivors, recovering the dead, and healing the physically and spiritually wounded was organized.

By the morning after the bombing, everything but the rescue efforts seemed to have slowed to half-speed. People spoke in low voices or silently greeted each other with spontaneous hugs. Various configurations of ribbons began to appear for the dead, the children, the families.

Newspapers and magazines around the world had published a photograph taken moments after the explosion. It was a policeman handing a dying baby to a rescue worker. The amateur photographer told me he spent the night in prayer and that he hoped the child's parents wouldn't be upset with him for such a heartbreaking image.

The rescue worker, a member of the Oklahoma City Fire Department, said that at the end of his long shift he called his wife to say he was

okay, and asked to talk to his son. He just wanted to hear his voice. We both had to pause before continuing the interview.

Oklahoma City is a modern capital with frontier-village sensibilities, and church is a big part of that. Nearly everyone I talked to raised the solace they sought in prayers or spoke of a victim as someone in their church or the relative of someone in their friend's church.

And there, on the prairie, there were no hiding places from the terrible reality of that cold-blooded act. The Alfred P. Murrah Federal Building was like an open casket standing on end, framed against the flat horizon. People would stand at a distance and quietly stare. It was impossible to ignore but equally difficult to comprehend.

Yet for all of the work at hand, for all of the grief and anxiety, Oklahoma City didn't set aside its manners. Heroes showed up on time for interviews and then to give credit to others. Politicians were bipartisan in their efforts and in the praise.

Our NBC News headquarters was a family electronics business badly damaged by the blast. We struck a deal for a temporary lease, but the next day the owner said he didn't feel right taking money on such an occasion. He also shared with us his favorite barbecue caterer, and brought his wife and grandchildren around. We set up computers in his accounting department and editing machines in his storage area. He simply went out of business for a week so we could stay on the air.

Through family and friends, I have always had a soft spot for Oklahoma. From Will Rogers, Jim Thorpe, Mickey Mantle, and Reba McEntire to *The Grapes of Wrath*, the musical *Oklahoma!* to Sooner football, oil-rich and dirt-poor, it's earned its place in American folklore as cowboy-tough and proudly self-reliant. Oklahomans may feel more vulnerable now, a little disoriented by what's happened to them, but in their response to this madness, they have elevated us all with their essential sense of goodness, community, and compassion.

VANTAGE POINT
The area around the site had become a city within a city, a war zone. At its edge, people gathered offering aid, trying to explain, reflecting on the pain.

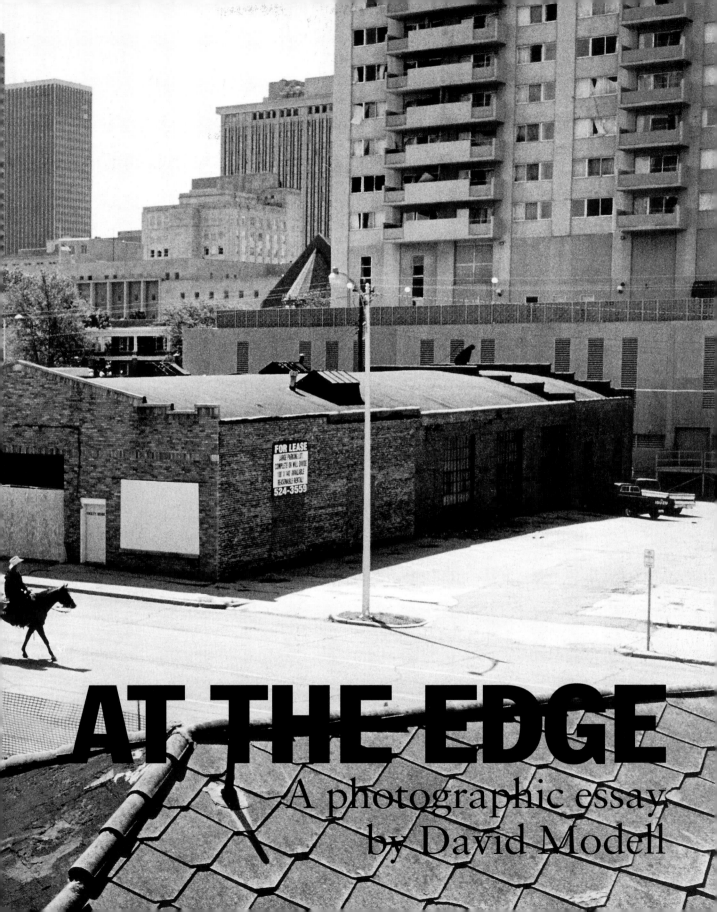

FOR LEASE
LARGE PARKING LOT
COMPLETE OR WILL DIVIDE
TOE ½ 140 AVAILABLE
REASONABLE RENTAL
524-3559

AT THE EDGE
A photographic essay
by David Modell

AFTERSHOCK
Some survivors came downtown with food and
flashlights; some with video cameras and
sandwiches; some with one another.

A SOLDIER'S GLORY
In contrast to the many children laid to rest with toys and teddy bears, a federal agent is buried at Rose Hill Cemetery with full military honors.

HEARTLAND
After the national prayer service, held on April 23, thousands of rural Oklahomans flocked to the perimeter of the bomb site.

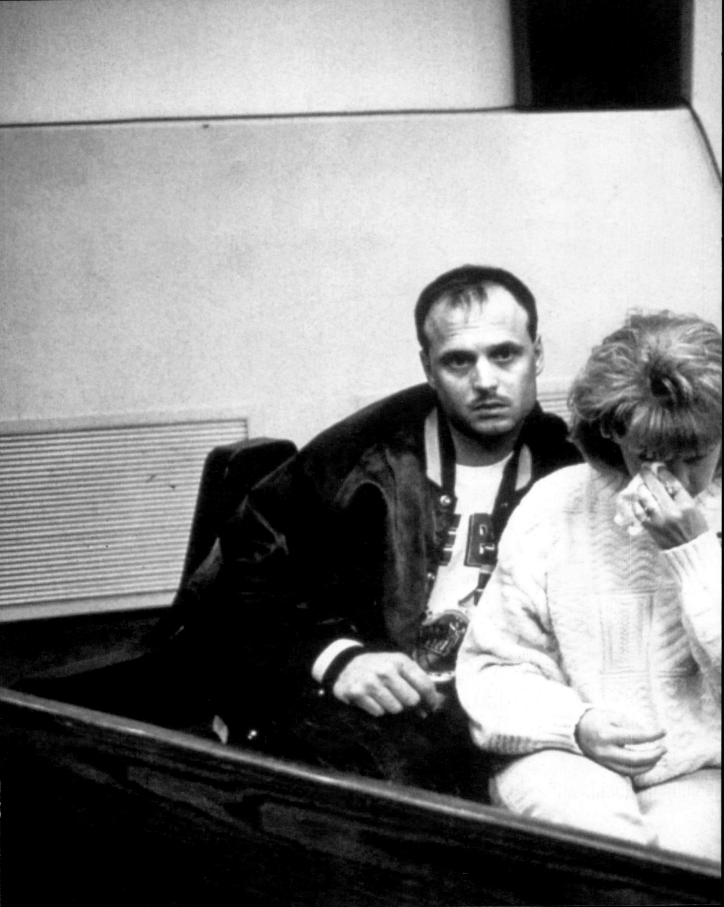

LORD OF MERCY
"There is no circumstance beyond God's ability to heal," one preacher said; this couple, attending a service at Eagle Heights Church two days after the bombing, are among the many who prayed it was so.

A COMING TOGETHER

"It's like the world ought to be"

Late on the evening of April 19, Cathy Keating felt the wave of frustration coming from the site. People were not being rescued quickly. Oklahoma's first lady decided that there had to be something to bind together the spirit of the community as it grappled with the tragedy. It was 11:00 P.M. when she asked her chief of staff, Barbie Jobe, to come over to the Governor's Mansion. At a meeting in the upstairs family room, with a handful of other aides and friends, she planned a prayer service. Mrs. Keating wanted it to be ecumenical, a place where everybody could find their own way to prayer. It would be called "A Time of Healing." They wanted to hold it on Friday evening, but the only suitable venue, the State Fair Arena, was taken up with an agricultural show, complete with dirt floor.

The ideal catalyst for the service, Mrs. Keating believed, would be the Reverend Billy Graham. Although he was due at the Mayo Clinic the following Monday and was not feeling well, the Reverend Graham immediately agreed to fly to Oklahoma. Sunday was fixed as the day, which meant that President and Mrs. Clinton would also be able to attend. In the few days available to organize the service, the impact of the tragedy on the whole nation became clear. In cities, towns, and villages flags flew at half-mast. Oklahomans no longer felt alone with their grief. People had been talking about the state's broken heart. But by the time arrangements for the prayer service were complete, the upwelling support, tangible in the out-of-state rescue teams and in messages pouring in from all over the country (and, indeed, the world), transformed the mood into one of extraordinary national bonding.

At 3:30 A.M. on Sunday a young woman called Jodee Walker, from southwestern Oklahoma, was the first to arrive at the arena, nearly twelve hours before the service was due to begin. Soon after dawn, she gave up first place in line to five-year-old Bradley Gooch, who was complaining of the cold after arriving at 7:00 A.M. with his aunt, Kathy Burt. Eventually, long lines of people encircled the arena. When the doors opened, nearly 19,000 people were waiting. One of them, Tracy McConnell of Oklahoma City, seemed to speak for all of them when she said, "Everyone's together like the world ought to be."

Those who could not get into the arena—as many as 30,000—were able to see and listen to the service on monitors in the grounds outside. Inside,

The idea of distributing bears to bereaved families for comfort came from Brenda Edgars, the first lady of Illinois. When the last consignment of the six hundred bears needed arrived, on Sunday morning, the Secret Service was sealing off the State Fair Arena. Even stuffed animals are subject to search, and every one was scanned. The ribbon is one of hundreds made by victims' families to thank rescue workers, from a design conceived by schoolchildren. Blue represents Oklahoma and purple is for children who died (yellow was also worn for those who were still missing).

TRAIL OF TEARS
Thousands gathered for the national prayer service held at the State Fair Arena on the Sunday morning after the bombing; those who could not get in to see the service went to a nearby baseball field and listened to it over loudspeakers.

IN UNISON
Waiving fees and union contracts, the Oklahoma City Philharmonic, the Canterbury Chorale, and vocalists Susan Powell and Kurt Johnson filled the stadium with sound.

SHARING THE SOLACE
Hillary Rodham Clinton, President Clinton, and Governor and Mrs. Keating flank Jason Smith and Dan McKinney, son and husband of Secret Service employee Linda McKinney. "My heart was torn apart by a coward's bomb," Dan later wrote, "but the memories will be everlasting."

some of the loudest applause went to rescue workers who appeared after a backstage meeting with President Clinton and attorney general Janet Reno. When President and Mrs. Clinton took their places, they were joined by Jason Smith and Dan McKinney, the son and husband of Secret Service agent Laura McKinney, who had worked in the Federal Building. Her body had not yet been found. To the left of Dan McKinney were Cathy Keating and Governor Frank Keating. Jason and Dan were clutching the symbolic ribboned teddy bears; as a hymn was sung, Cathy Keating felt directly the emotional response of Dan and his son—grief, sorrow, and relief, a catharsis shared with many other families in the arena at that moment.

Billy Graham's own commitment to the suffering was palpable. As well as bearing sympathy, he reinforced the sense of moral outrage and the desire for justice and for the perpetrators to pay the cost: "Someday those who thought they could sow chaos and discord will be brought to justice," he said (a theme echoed by speakers representing other denominations and by the President). There was a force in Graham's voice that galvanized the whole arena. He seemed to find new strength as he gripped the podium. And as he stepped down, his wife, Ruth, patted his hand. The man with the ever-noble head of the evangelist had found within himself enough strength to pass on to the thousands who heard him. The President, who on April 19 had said the bombing "was an act of

Chad Roy Harris, five, helps keep night vigil in a field in Stillwater.

cowardice and it was evil," linked justice with faith and talked of "dark forces that threaten our common peace, our freedom, our way of life." Rabbi David Packman, of Temple B'nai Israel, cited the biblical cities that were destroyed forever—Babylon, Nineveh—but likened Oklahoma to Jerusalem, which had been restored "more beautiful, more holy, more together."

The most astonishing, soaring consummation of the spirit of healing came, appropriately, in a finale watched by millions on national television. Few in the arena, or anywhere else, knew who Ernestine Dillard was as she rose to sing "God Bless America." She had been chosen too late to be named in the program. (Afterward, hundreds called *The Daily Oklahoman* to find out her name.)

And, in fact, Dillard had led a comfortably obscure life until about a year before the prayer service. Then a friend told her that God wanted Ernestine to enter an "American Traditions" singing contest in Savannah, Georgia. She walked away the winner, which came as no surprise to those who knew her singing back at her home church in Bixby, near Tulsa. Since then, Dillard had sung with the Tulsa Philharmonic and at Governor Keating's inauguration. She is a registered nurse, and the prayer service appealed to her maternal emotions. She was, she told a reporter, the mother of "about ten children—three are left at home. Some are biological, some mixed-family, others adopted."

PRESIDENT CLINTON:

Let us let our own children know that we will stand against the forces of fear. When there is talk of hatred, let us stand up and talk against it. When there is talk of violence, let us stand up and talk against it. In the face of death, let us honor life. As St. Paul admonished us, let us not be overcome by evil, but overcome evil with good.

THE REVEREND BILLY GRAHAM:

A tragedy like this could have torn this city apart, but instead it has united this city and you have become a family. We have seen people coming together in a way we never could have imagined, and that is an example to us all. Hundreds if not thousands of prayer groups across the nation have arisen to pray for Oklahoma City.

The forces of hate and violence must not be allowed to gain their victory, not just in our society, but in our hearts. Nor must we respond to hate with more hate. This is a time of coming together, and we have seen that and been inspired by it.

GOVERNOR FRANK KEATING:

Never in the history of our country have Americans witnessed such senseless barbarism. It has been suggested that those who committed this act of mass murder chose us as their victims because we were supposedly immune—the heartland of America.

Well, we are the heartland of America. Today we stand before the world, and before our God, together—our hearts and hands linked in a solidarity these criminals can never understand. We stand together in love.

THROUGH CHILDREN'S EYES

Messages of love and generosity

Thirty children were orphaned by the bombing. Another 219 were left with only one parent. Not only in Oklahoma, but all over the United States, schoolchildren reacted to the tragedy in a way that seemed like an exercise in national group therapy. Many children were encouraged to send messages to Oklahoma, and hundreds of these poured into the office of the Governor. Some of them follow. But first, a glimpse of one child's compassion for others in Oklahoma City itself:

Police lieutenant Jim W. Spearman was standing guard at the perimeter of the bomb site:
It was about 3:00 A.M. and cold, windy, and wet. Because of the weather, we were taking turns standing outside, and this was my turn. I noticed three people standing just north of the barricade: a boy in his mid-teens, a younger girl, and a woman. I thought it was very strange for that time of morning, especially in that weather. The boy walked toward me and asked if his sister could

talk to me. The woman prompted the little girl, who looked about nine. She handed me a well-worn teddy bear and asked, "Could you give this to one of those babies in the hospital?"

The woman explained that the little girl hadn't been sleeping well since the bombing and was very concerned about the child victims. She had woken about an hour before and asked if she could go to the bomb site. The bear had been given to her around her first birthday. I told her that I would take it to the Salvation Army post, and they would make sure that one of the children in the hospital got it. When I asked the little girl what her name was, she said, "That's not important."

Joy Morris is a seventh grader at Cooper Middle School, in northwest Oklahoma City:
At 9:02 A.M. on April 19 I felt the school shake. Sometime later, we were all called out into the commons area and the television was turned on. Immediately, we saw horrible, unedited pictures of

Dear Governor
Keating,

I am Five years old
and This is my
Favorite stuffed
animal. I Thought
you might know a
Little Boy or girl
who needs it More
Than I do. I send
it with Love.

Love,
Annie
Polcari

Eric's Dream
by Eric Baker

I dreamed that all the babies and people that died in the explosion came down from heaven to help fix the buildings and find all the victims and survivors. They helped people's hearts so they could build the buildings the way they were before the bomb. Then they brought down roses on their wings so they could be planted all around in honor of the victims, the Firemen, the rescue workers and all the friends that helped.

They stayed until it was done. And as they left the babies told the people to never let this happen again.

Eric Charles Baker
age 10
Norman, Oklahoma

We send our love and pray that all will soon be well.

Lisa Smith

I LAV YU

Our prayers and our hearts go out to all of you.

Shana O'Brien

I CARE FOR YOU

LOVE LETTERS
The post-disaster deluge of correspondence received by Governor Keating's office included these panels, which comprised part of an enormous banner sent by a Montessori school in Maryland.

destruction. As the day continued, the school's population decreased as students left with their parents and family members. I heard that both parents of a student had been in the building and were hospitalized, and another student's parents were reported missing. The next day at school, everyone was depressed, and I learned of many more of my neighbors, classmates, and friends who were affected. One of my neighbors told me that her husband worked in the Federal Building and he, ironically, left for an out-of-town meeting just minutes before the explosion. Now all his co-workers were victims.

As the days passed, things only got worse. One week after the disaster, a special assembly was held at our school. Being a member of the band, I was part of that assembly. Students who knew the victims stood up and read letters to the rescue workers, and we played "America the Beautiful." As I played my flute, I got a special feeling, and I began to feel a little better about everything.

Danielle Reece, age eleven, wrote this letter shortly after the bombing. Virgil Reece, her father, is the area real estate manager for Southwestern Bell Telephone, whose holdings include eight buildings that were damaged. As a result, Mr. Reece was needed at the site for several consecutive days. Too emotional to read Danielle's words at the time, he shared her letter with members of Sacramento's TF-7 Fire & Rescue unit, who carried copies with them during their stay:
April 22, 1995

I Love You! DaD, though I may not tell you all the time, I Love you very very much. I'm sorry I wrote you But I can't tell you to your Face Because it would make me cry. But, It makes me cry after I talk to you on the phone or see you drive away. I think It is so Bad what those men did. I guess I'm

being selfish But I want you at home with me & mom & dawn we miss you very much. I now that all those workers people need your help but I do to Because your my daddy your spost to Be there to pretekt me from everything & I now that you wont alwas be with me but I need you now. I guess I should Be usto it by know Because you usaly gone on a bussnes trip or sopmething. I Love you so much I can't cry or talk to mom or Dawn. So during the day I walk out to the Big trackter & cry then to dry the tearse I ride my bike it calms me down Before I go inside. I guess this is like a small portion of what kids that parents are devoresd are like but in some ways it's not Because you call & come home sometimes & mom told me not to make you feel gilty about this hole thing Because it wasn't your fault & I now that & I Dont want It to sound like that OK. I Love you Come home as soon as you can. I will pray for you If you will pray for me! Love (heart) Danielle Reece

Tia Ketner is thirteen. Her grandmother, Linda "Coleen" Housley, worked and died in the credit union at the Federal Building:
On April 19 I returned home from school, running in happy. My mom had tears running from her eyes and she sat me down and explained that my Grandma Housely had been in the explosion. She was innocent, sweet, and loving. I had never lost anyone before. I didn't understand how someone you loved could die. All we could do was wait...and wait. Nine grandchildren, three grown children, two-stepkids, two sons-in-law, a daughter-in-law, a loving husband of nineteen months, two sisters—many churches were involved in the waiting and hoping. All the support was wonderful, but not enough. All we wanted was my grandma back, safe and alive. Finally on Tuesday, they found my grandma, not

alive and unharmed, but brittle. She had died immediately.

The funeral was Thursday; it was beautiful. I thought of the kids and the others who died. To lose a grandma or friend is a great tragedy, but to lose a child or mother or dad is probably the worst—a mother or father who had loved and raised you for a long time, or a child who has barely begun to live his life. I wish I could go door-to-door and apologize to everyone who lost someone, but I can't.

Mike Miller is a police captain in Ada, Oklahoma: A Red Cross worker gave me a bag of candy from a little girl called Melia. When I opened it I found, along with the candy, $1.15 and a note thanking me for my help. This brought tears to my eyes, knowing this little girl did the only thing she knew to do. I have three little girls at home and I know how important $1.15 is to them. That $1.15 will never be the spent and I will keep it and remember that little girl forever. A donation to the Red Cross was made in that little girl's name. May God bless and keep Melia all the days of her life.

Delphine Hensley is ten: My grandparents flew out of Cleveland, Ohio, Saturday morning after the bombing. A man in a blue uniform and his dog boarded the plane and sat across from them. His name was Gary Brogerg. He worked with FEMA, and his dog's name was Bo. My grandparents were really happy that someone would come all the way from Cleveland, Ohio, to help out, and when we met them at the Oklahoma City airport, they insisted that we would drop him off downtown at the building. Then they invited him to stay with them and gave him rides to and from the bomb site. Gary stayed with my grandparents all his time in Oklahoma City. My grandma is a great cook, and she made sure he had good meals, hot showers, and a good bed to sleep in. My grandparents are animal lovers too, so yes, you guessed it, Bo also had good meals and a good bed to sleep on—it was the king-size one in the extra room. Bo liked the cats, and the cats did not mind Bo.

Trudy Stillwell White is an eighth grade teacher at St. Charles Borromeo Catholic School, in northwest Oklahoma City. The children in her class had sent lunch sacks to the rescuers, filled with snacks and messages. In addition to their many cards, they also sent a banner.
Our entire community was touched by the tragedy. Three members of our parish family were killed in the explosion. Teachers attended funerals, older students were asked to be altar servers, and our school cafeteria was used for a funeral dinner.

So, a week and a day after the bomb, we were trying to restore some normalcy to the school. There was a knock at the side door. Four imposing figures, ATF agents wearing their helmets and their uniforms, walked in. They had been cheered by our cards, had read the prayers and thoughts on our banner, and had eaten our snacks. They had come to say thank you. We assembled the children in the cafeteria.

When the ATF agents entered, after a hushed moment, the children jumped to their feet and burst into cheers. One of the agents removed himself from the crowd and sat silent and alone, his face haggard with fatigue and sorrow. A group of eighth grade girls saw him and wrote a card with the words "We Love You" in bold Magic Marker. They shyly approached the agent and handed him the card. He began to cry.

ENCOURAGING WORDS

"I just want to let you know that you have to stay strong through the hard times," wrote one Missouri child to "everyone in Oklahoma City." "We love you because you save people," a class in Bristol, Connecticut, wrote. "It must be very hard to do so much digging."

DAYS OF GRIEF

First, one rose, then a hundred

At 10:00 A.M. eastern time on April 26, one week after the bombing, the bells of St. Patrick's Cathedral in New York City rang out, and as the moment moved across the time zones of America, so the bells of other cathedrals, other churches, other chapels rang out, too. Outside the Murrah Building the cranes lifting concrete debris stopped. At 9:02 A.M. Governor Frank Keating blew a whistle and then the only sound was that of the Oklahoman and American flags flapping as they hung on the wrecked building. There was a minute of silence to remember the dead: those accounted for and those yet to be found. There were many to grieve for, and the grief showed on the faces of the rescuers, too. When it came time for Oklahoma City to bid farewell to them, on Friday, May 5, the act of closure became a communal rite of passage.

These hours are reported by Mike Brake, chief writer to Governor Keating:
The final scoops of rubble rattled into bins at 11:58 P.M. on Thursday, May 4. Only three bodies remained unrecovered. Deputy fire chief Jon Hansen's midnight press briefing put the ultimate death toll at 166 (it would be eventually 168).

"We'll place a wreath, and then we'll be gone," Hansen said.

The rescuers gathered for a final time on the afternoon of May 5, fourteen hours after the site was released to local authorities. They jammed the street in front of the building and mustered in ragged formations on the scorched parking lot across the street, talking and hugging and crying in their uniforms and windbreakers and medical smocks. As the 2:00 P.M. ceremony neared, they added red roses to the mound of flowers at the west end of the building, where a makeshift shrine stood beneath a leaning wedge of concrete bearing the words, in red spray paint, "BLESS THE CHILDREN + THE INNOCENT."

A blue child's balloon bobbed between the Oklahoman and American flags. Stuffed bears peeked from the floral displays, and bits of poetry mounded on the shattered sidewalk. One bear wore a pair of white baby shoes and held a card: "You will never be forgotten." A wreath from NBC News overlapped one bearing the Marine Corps motto, *Semper Fi.* A scuffed plaque bore the photo of a Little League team, the Bluejays, 1990 champs from Midwest City. A small stuffed dog wore a Red Cross sticker: "Help Can't Wait."

REACHING THE PLACE
On May 6, no longer barred from where their loved ones died, three thousand mourners brought mementos, tears, and prayers to the Federal Building, and the site became a shrine.

ENDLESS HOURS
The children of HUD employee Castine Deveroux wait at home for news of their mother. One week later, she was buried from St. John Missionary Baptist Church.

At 1:37 the Oklahoma City Police Honor Guard formed ranks in front of a makeshift podium set atop rough plywood, directly over the bomb crater. The medical examiner's staff, in their green and white lab coats, gathered to the left. Agents from the FBI and ATF formed to the right. More than a dozen different uniforms dotted the crowd of a thousand.

The sound of drums and bagpipes echoed off the windowless Journal Record Building at 1:56, and the band approached from the southeast, rounding the corner of the building at a slow cadence. As the pipers played "Amazing Grace," a dozen men and women in different uniforms placed a large wreath in front of the shrine. They formed a circle, holding hands, a National Guardsman in camouflage and a firefighter in an orange-billed cap flanking a blond FBI agent. The pipes echoed through the building's shell.

As fire and police buglers Jerry Aduddell and Terry Turner played "Taps," the rescuers moved slowly, spontaneously toward the red tape in front of the pit. First, one rose sailed into the rubble, then a dozen, then a hundred. The floral carpet grew and spread. One Native American policeman gave two barking tribal yells. A tall ATF agent threw his rose high into the swirling breeze; it settled on a ragged outcropping of cement. He turned and hugged a tiny firefighter, who shredded the petals from her rose and scattered them into the pit.

They were all moving forward now, the Salvation Army and Red Cross workers, the deputies and marshals and special agents and sergeants, to add their roses. It was a salute, a farewell, and an apology, too, to those they couldn't save. For many who witnessed it, the moment was the most dignified and moving of their lives. For the rescuers, it was over.

The families came on Saturday, after a night of steady rain. They arrived in buses at the east gate,

where pastors and counselors and Red Cross volunteers welcomed them with boxes of tissues and hugs. A double line of orange barricades marked a path across the Journal Record Building's parking lot to a tented shrine at the west end.

Few of the family members had seen the building. As they moved down the path they stopped to stare, to point, to weep, or to gasp. Many snapped photos. Some took twenty minutes to walk the hundred-odd paces from the bus to the tent. In front of the pit, along a muddy strip pavement, the families paused to take bits of rubble from plastic pails, snap photos, point, and whis-

per. Discreetly, the two sons of Virginia Thompson, one of three people left buried in the final pile, were allowed to stand by the rubble. "I remember walking on roses...walking on roses to get to where they thought Mom was," said Ken Thompson. Rosemary Koelsch, whose daughter, Valerie, had worked in the third-floor credit union, stood at the red tape, four feet from the bomb crater. She wore a large metal button with Valerie's picture: Valerie is smiling, leaning forward, in a blouse and multicolored vest. It's the kind of snapshot you take at a family gathering—a birthday party or christening. "Where that yellow bucket is, there in

the third floor, that's where Valerie's desk was," Rosemary said. "That door behind, I came through that door a hundred times." The morning's clouds had rolled off to the east, unveiling blue skies. Rosemary shielded her eyes against the now-bright sun, pursed her lips, took a final look. And then she walked away, through puddles to the idling buses.

Larry Collins is a fire captain who was dispatched to Oklahoma City by FEMA:
One night I was stopped by a man who explained that his five-year old daughter had something to tell me. The little girl stood behind him, clinging to his leg. "Go ahead, honey," he said as she stepped forward. I got down on one knee to be at her eye level. Then she held out something in her little hand. It was a gold angel-of-mercy pin with a colored ribbon signifying the children lost in the bombing. In a halting voice, barely audible, she said, "This is to protect you and your friends while you look for our friends." After I hugged her and thanked her, she stepped back to her father. I did not know what to say. Later that night I walked out of the Murrah Building and stopped at a shrine of flowers and stuffed animals placed in front of the heap where

OFFICIAL MOURNING
Police officers Phillip Moffit (left) and Olan Boydston see Baylee Almon laid to rest in their hometown of Spencer, Oklahoma.

eighty people were still buried. I felt a flood of emotion as I remembered that innocent little girl. Next to the flowers and bandaged teddy bears I spray-painted a prayer on a broken concrete slab: "BLESS THE CHILDREN + THE INNOCENT."

Randy Dunn is the uncle of Karan Denise Shepherd, who worked for the credit union. Her body was found on April 30:
After the pastor concluded Karan's funeral service and friends filed by the family, I noticed this uniformed firefighter standing just outside the tent, waiting his turn to express his sorrow to Karan's mother. I extended my hand to him and told him of our family's gratitude to him and his fellows for the tough job they had done. I noticed sorrow in his eyes. The next day we learned that the young man had been the one who recovered Karan's body. This man showed the depth of his character by staying with my niece to the very end, and never claimed any of the credit or love our family believes he deserves.

Wallace J. Graves is a fire marshal from Dallas, Texas. He volunteered to help in Oklahoma City:
We were not the heroes everybody tried to claim we were. The true heroes are the people of Oklahoma. They endured an extremely traumatic assault on their community and came back fighting with every tool they had. They demonstrated courage, love, and compassion for their fellow man in a way the United States has rarely seen. The "Okies" taught the nation a lesson in bravery. I am proud to be married to an Okie.

Captain Edward A. Greene is with California's FEMA Task Force III:
Lieutenant Stockton joined us for lunch and brought a single red rose and a name on a piece of paper. A woman had asked him if he could get close to the building. He said that he could, and she said that her son, who was listed as missing, would be forty-three years old on that day and she would like to have the rose placed in an appropriate spot in the building. She wanted to have someone wish him a happy birthday for her. I took the flower directly to assistant chief Mike Shannon of the Oklahoma City Fire Department, and later he confirmed that it had been put in the midst of the concrete slabs. I could see it resting there, a bright red symbol of hope and love surrounded by the destruction, in the exact spot where the woman's son was found that morning, on his forty-third birthday.

Michael Blazi is a volunteer who was assigned to bus duty on the day the families of victims were allowed to see the Federal Building:
I noticed a family of an older man and woman, a younger woman, and a boy, probably in his late teens. The family's son, husband, and father had been found, unearthed and identified earlier in the week. Now, I saw the boy standing by himself in front of fire chief Marrs. The Chief was in front of the rubble pile, available to answer any questions the families might have. A yellow-and-black crime scene tape separated the boy and the chief. The two men, one of them black, young, tall, and wiry and weary with grief, and the other one, white, middle-aged, short, and stocky and weary with many weights, looked at each other. They just stared at each other. Then the boy, towering over the Chief, leaned toward him. The Chief raised his arms over the tape to meet the boy in an embrace. This was not a quick pat-on-the-back hug that said, "It'll be okay," but an embrace of strength and sorrow that said, "This isn't okay. It won't be for a long time, and I thank you all the more because of it."

FACING LOSS
A woman who has lost a loved one holds close to her child and her faith.

REMAKING LIVES

"The loss you feel must not paralyze your own lives"

The emotional wounds of the Oklahoma bombing were spread far wider than the physical wounds. The first critical problem facing counselors was that as long as bodies remained unrecovered, the kin of the missing could not accept that they were dead. During a search lasting two weeks, the confirmation of deaths was slow and random. Families of the victims were gathered in two places, the downtown Red Cross headquarters and the First Christian Church. A strict cordon was established between the families and the media. This followed a new regimen for dealing with disasters, the result of lessons learned in other places. But this was not like Hurricane Andrew or the Californian earthquakes, where family counseling had been refined. Here, the carnage had been inflicted in seconds and was concentrated in one place; it had taken lives indiscriminately from a highly diverse group. If anyone recognized the problems peculiar to such a catastrophe, it was Victoria Cummock.

Victoria Cummock: Tell it as it is.

In 1988 Victoria had lost her husband on Pan Am 103 over Lockerbie, Scotland. Then, the handling of family members looking for survivors had been a gruesome fiasco (the flight manifest was released to the press before the victims' families were notified). Victoria had three children, ages three, four, and six. The personal hell she went through in the following months converted her to the cause of family counseling, and when she saw the Oklahoma bombing on TV, she recognized all too well what its consequences would be for the grieving families. She faxed a letter to a senior White House aide, Bruce Lindsey, stressing how vital it was to provide skilled counseling in Oklahoma City. President Clinton saw this letter just as he was working on the speech he would make at the Oklahoma prayer service. He quoted directly from Virginia's letter:

"The anger you feel is valid, but you must not allow yourselves to be consumed by it. The hurt you feel must not be allowed to turn into hate, but instead into the search for justice. The loss you feel must not paralyze your own lives. Instead, you must try to pay tribute to your loved ones by continuing to do all the things they left undone, thus ensuring they did not die in vain." Afterward, the President phoned Victoria at her home in Coral Gables, Florida, to thank her. She told him she was ready to go to Oklahoma City to help, and within hours she had been sponsored by the Red Cross. Once in Oklahoma City, Victoria joined other counselors at the First Christian Church. She went into overdrive, working sixteen-hour days.

"I wasn't prepared for the devastation," she said, "nor do I hope I would ever be." Her advice was influential at a critical moment nearly two weeks after the bombing. On May 1 there were reports—false, as it turned out—that the rescuers were calling off the search for bodies because the building was too dangerous.

Governor Keating and fire chief Marrs went to the church in order to reassure the families who had still not had their kin recovered that the rescue work was, in fact, continuing. The Governor and the Chief were uncertain how they should describe the realities of the search. Chief Marrs brought a plan of the Murrah Building indicating where they thought the remaining bodies were located.

Before the two men faced the families, they sought advice from the counselors. Some of the most forceful advice came from Victoria Cummock. She told them to disregard the rumors—and argued that the families were so fragmented that it was a waste of time to deny something that they would not, in any case, be aware of. Instead, she said, "Say, 'This is the straight story, the truth.' And understand that the next question they will ask is, 'What about the condition of the bodies?'"

One question hung in the air: Would everybody be accounted for? It was impossible to answer at that time (the medical examiner's identification rate was more than any had dared hope for).

The Governor and the Chief then went down the hall to a large room where the families were gathered. They spanned every generation—brothers, sisters, fathers, mothers, grandparents—and

Fire Chief Gary Marrs: an embrace

every background. Almost immediately, the Governor was asked if there was any chance of anyone now being found alive. Going as far as he felt able, he said, "The chance is very, very remote."

Chief Marrs, acutely feeling the emotions of the family room, was careful and precise about the situation in the building. He explained that the hardest bodies to reach were where several floors had fallen and been compressed into the "pancake." He produced the plan followed by the rescuers, and after he had spoken, several groups of people pored over it. Then a young

Native American woman, clearly distressed, went up to the Chief and hugged him and said that she wanted to say, on behalf of everyone in the room, how grateful they felt for the way in which the rescuers were risking their lives. At that moment, the Chief and the Governor were subsumed into the family of the grieving. Everyone in the room held hands and prayed.

Victoria Cummock had made the point, talking to the families, that they were dealing with a case of mass murder. She had no patience with euphemisms. Someone in her own family had said, of her husband, that "John had passed away." "Acknowledge what it is," Victoria said, "or you're never going to help anybody. If people don't get outraged by murder, then the system doesn't change." Sometime later, family members would come up to her and say, earnestly, "You understand that this was murder, don't you?"

She insisted on harsher terms because, she said, people were not going to be able to deal with their feelings unless they dealt with realities. "Six and a half years after Pan Am 103," she said, "those who didn't get psychological help are still in the anger stage. Everybody lives differently and grieves differently. By articulating in the most truthful way, you are helping them to choose the right thing for them."

The healing would take a long while. Without the bodies of their loved ones, many of the families were still in denial. "But," said Victoria, "as the camera lights go off, the media goes away, and everybody goes back to their lives, these people

don't have the same life to go back to. The devastation is going to start now for them."

Tamara E. Varga is a speech-and-language pathologist who coordinated the family room at the First Christian Church:

The family room was more than just a place where families received information; it was a little piece of home for some. The families began to pull together and support each other. They made the ribbons with angel-of-mercy pins that were given to all rescue workers. One morning a rescue worker mislaid his ribbon and reportedly tore his place apart until he found it. Families truly helped each other. Several who had already been notified about the death of their loved ones came back to spend time supporting others still waiting to hear something. It touched me to see the strength they showed by reaching out to someone else when they themselves had lost so much. On April 26, 1995, one week after the bombing, the moment of silence was shared among those in the family room at 9:02 A.M. As tears streamed down my face, a mother, waiting to hear if her child had survived, took my hand and said, "Good will come from this. Please hold that in your heart." She released my hand and when I looked up she was gone. I know she was right because so much good had already happened right here in the family room.

Rhonda Harris is a therapist who went to the First Christian Church to escort families of victims:

My partner and I were asked to type a form that would be used by the families to record information about their loved ones. I turned on the computer and the screen read, "Enter password." Oh no, I thought, just what I needed. Then my partner yelled, "I got it." "What did you type?" I

asked. She replied, "I typed in God." I knew at this moment that we were not alone.

Karen Bacon was at the First Christian Church:
A little boy, who looked around nine or ten, came up, talked to me, and kept wanting to help. I knew by the sticker on his name tag he had an immediate family member missing. I told him it was okay, he didn't need to help. His reply was, "I've got to do something. It's driving me crazy just sitting here." I think his name was Brett. He helped unload donations and bring things in from outside. Anything we asked, he did. When it was time to go home, I took him up to another volunteer, explained everything, and the last time I saw him he was following her.

Harry W. Allison counseled family members after they had been notified of a death:
After several hours the families would recover sufficiently to leave the First Christian Church. We did not see them again—with one exception. I had driven from Tulsa that day and noted that all the cars coming toward me had their headlights on, in honor of the victims, and I did likewise. Ten hours later, when I returned to my car, the battery was dead. A tall black man who was with a white lady approached me, saw that the hood of my car was up, and said familiarly, "Why, Doc, you've got car trouble. I'll get my car and get you jump-started." Then I recognized them as a couple I had seen earlier in the church. I said, "It wasn't more than an hour ago you were notified that you lost your two little children...and you want to help me?" He pulled the photos of his two boys from his breast pocket and said, "We're all in this together. We're all in this together, Doc." The words to the old song "Amazing Grace" keep recurring in my mind. Amazing Grace...

AN AMERICAN FAMILY

Who were they, those who died? The bomb took from all of us

By Tish Durkin

The bomb played no favorites; its brutality was blind. Raymond Lee Johnson, a son of the Seminole nation, perished with Adele Higginbottom, a Daughter of the American Revolution; Charlotte Thomas and Lakesha Levy, descendants of African-born slaves, died with Emilio Tapia, now laid to rest back home in Mexico.

Virginia Thompson, fifty-six, who sat down at the reception desk of the Federal Employees Credit Union every morning by eight o'clock died, with just-transferred Secret Service agent Alan Whicher, forty, who was planning a weekend trip with his family to explore their new home state of Oklahoma, and Tevin Garret, one, who loved to slide down his red-and-blue slide (head first).

"This terrible sin took the lives of our American family," said the President, "innocent children...citizens in the building going about their daily business...those who served the rest of us."

He was right: Cartney Jean McRaven, nineteen years old and married four days, had gone to the Social Security office to change her surname...Donna and Robert Luster, Jr., middle-aged and financially strapped, were in search of disability funds to feed their six children...LaRue and Luther Treanor were coming to see about Luther's retirement, which he was going to spend raising cattle. "We had the crazy idea Limousins would do good," says their son, Brad. "Dad had a lot of red Angus, too."

Planted in hatred of the government, the bomb landed among the people who served that government at its least exalted, most familiar level; people who worked in cubicles and stuck to their lunch hours, who made best efforts, modest livings, and small splashes. People whose real lives lay far from the Alfred P. Murrah Federal Building.

They were mothers; mothers, in many cases, whose children knew no other parent. Eleven-year-old Jonmichael Rigney's father took off before he was born, but not his mother. Whether Trudy Rigney was stumbling, for a time, into a homeless shelter or rising to work at the Water Resources Board and study at the university, "Jonmichael was right at her heels," remembers her brother, Rick. "They were mother and son, but it was best buddies, too."

They were fathers; standard-issue American dads who knew they were strong and thought they were funny:

"Sara, if you will mow the lawn every weekend this summer, I will give you the keys to a brand new Honda," Social Security employee Steve Williams once promised his daughter.

"What's the catch?"

"No catch."

"I jumped up from the couch and peered out the back door," recalls Sara. "A lawn mower—a brand new Honda lawn mower."

They were neighbors and colleagues and goofballs from way back when: "I have known my very best friend since our days in Little League," writes Scott Moore of Scott Williams, twenty-four. "I will miss his cheerful face, his cheesy mustache, and his endless love of all sports."

They were shadows and echoes, by way of spouses. "We had begun to think and look alike," says Barbara Burns of herself and Donald, her husband of thirty-two years, "as some people say you do after you've been together for so long."

They were, as preschoolers and Social Security customers tend to be, family to one another:

America's Kids director Dana Cooper, twenty-four, and her son, Christopher, two. Cheryl Hammons, forty-four, and her grandchildren, Peachlyn Bradley, three, and Gabreon Bruce, three months. Aaron Coverdale, five-and-a-half, and his brother, Elijah, three-and-a-half. Chase Smith, three, and his brother Colton, two. "Colton ate everything. People called him 'fat rat' and 'chunky monkey,'" says his mother, Edye Smith. "Chase was very courteous. He would open doors for women and say, 'Here you go, pretty lady.'"

They were, to use an old-fashioned phrase that fits, solid citizens. Gilberto Martinez, who ran the Hispanic Assembly of God Church, had taken Emilio Tapia to get a Social Security number. Thomas Hawthorne was trying to help a retired United Rubber Workers union member clear up a problem with his federal benefits.

But first and last, they were people like us. Ken Bolte loved hockey, the Razorbacks, and his new green Chevy Blazer. Jo Ann Whittenberg whipped up a mean Italian-cream-and-7-Up pound cake. Bob Walker had a houseful of Shriner and scouting stuff and computers all over the place.

They were.

Now, all of a sudden, they are angels. Angels, pinned to ribbons, marked the rescue workers; angels, fastened in memory to the people they have lost, inhabit the minds of their survivors. "Carol Louise Bowers was truly 'Our Angel,'" writes a friend. "She touched scores of individuals with her caring, courteous, compassionate manner."

"She always was the type of person to take care of others," her husband says of Kimberly Burgess, twenty-nine, "Just like an angel!"

"She was like an angel from God," says Deniece Bell of her fifteen-month-old daughter, Danielle. "She always had a smile on her face."

Their résumés are eulogies: "At the time of her death, Karen Gist Carr was an employee of the U.S. Army Recruiting Command, an instructor of aerobics at the downtown YMCA and a partner in an Amway distributorship…"

Their opinions have become last wishes. "I'm going to try to enroll Shane, our five-year-old son, in a private school, because that's what [Christy] really wanted," Chris Rosas told *The New York Times.* "We had some arguments about that." His wife, Christy, was twenty-two.

Their faith is glory, for these people lived and died believing. "It's hard to believe Jesus loves you more than we do," it says in the blue funeral booklet distributed for Kim Cousins at the South Lindsay Baptist Church, where she taught second grade Sunday School, "but He does! We will miss you, but only until the trumpet sounds…"

"I believe she carried some children from day care as they rose to be united with Our Heavenly Father," writes Terry Koelsch of his sister, Valerie. "I know she is playing with them right now."

Such was the power of the bomb: It made miraculous visions of people next door, and Armageddon of a workday, and a time to mourn of the spring.

It enshrined the past. "If we wanted to buy something or take a vacation to Hawaii, we did," writes Bruce Griffin, who lost his wife, Ethel. "And I thank God that we did realize that…there are no guarantees for tomorrow."

It erased the future. "My children will never get to meet him, to hear him, to feel him, or to love him," writes the daughter of Richard Allen.

It destroyed even the ones who survived. "My life will go on, but without joy, love, and fire," writes Charles H. Stratton, whose wife, Dee, was killed on a day that began like any other.

Along with Shelly Turner Bland, twenty-five, who would have been married one year this June.

And Antonio Cooper, six months old.

And Oleta Biddy, who, her husband Hank had predicted, "will not be found until the last baby is found. That is the way she would want it." And so it was.

On the last morning of her life, as she was getting out of her daughter Oneta's truck on the way to work, Norma Jean Johnson smiled and said, "Now, don't forget me."

Here, we remember them all.

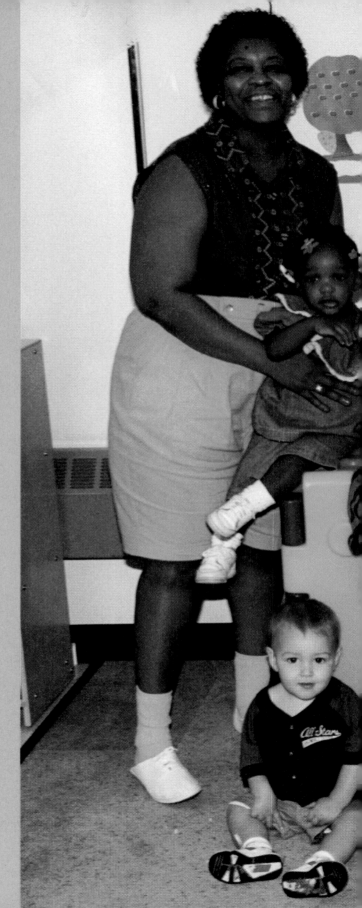

A SNAPSHOT WITH TEACHER
Brenda Daniels Marsh, left, was a teacher at the day-care center in the Federal Building. She died in the blast. So, too, did some of the children in this picture.

Lucio Aleman, Jr., 33, FHA;
husband of Gabriella,
father of Alynna and Lucio

Teresa Alexander, 33,
Social Security customer;
one husband, two jobs,
three children

Richard Allen, 46, Social Security;
"...beautiful, kind, pure,
and wholesome...,"
writes his daughter

Ted Allen, 48, HUD;
"My dad was tall—taller
than the buildings,"
says Austin Allen, 4

Baylee Almon, 1 year and 1 day;
buried where birds sing
and build their nests

Diane Althouse, 45, HUD;
four days away from vows
as a Benedictine Oblate novice

Rebecca Anderson, 37,
volunteer rescuer;
gave her life,
then donated her heart

Pamela Argo, 36,
Social Security customer;
she wore a black hat
and bright red lipstick

Sandy Avery, 34,
Social Security;
night student
of sign language

Peter Avillanoza, 56, HUD;
loved the music
of his native Hawaii

Danielle Nicole Bell, 15 months;
"that precious smile...,"
her mother remembers

Oleta Biddy, 54, Social Security;
"Well, hello there,"
was her famous greeting

Shelly Turner Bland, 25, DEA;
"Mommie, I miss you,"
writes Jordan Elizabeth, 4

Olen Bloomer, 61, USDA ;
"Big Dad"
to his grandchildren

James Boles, 50, USDA;
"An outstanding individual,"
says James Boles, 8

Mark Bolte, 28, FHA;
Boy Scout leader,
Knight of the Altar, golfer

Cassandra Booker, 25;
was applying for
Social Security cards
for two of her four children

Carol Bowers, 53, Social Security;
thirty-four years
on the job

Peachlyn Bradley, 3;
Social Security customer;
"Acted like she was 23,"
her aunt says

Woody Brady, 41,
Credit Union customer;
top of his class
at Meeker High

Cynthia Brown, 26,
Secret Service;
married her husband, Ron,
six weeks before she died

Paul Broxterman, 43, HUD;
moved to this office
two weeks before the bombing

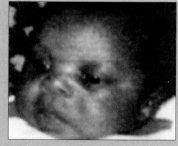

Gabreon Bruce, 3 months,
Social Security customer;
his mother was getting
a card for him

Kimberly Burgess, 29,
Credit Union;
helped older members
balance their checkbooks

David Burkett, 47, HUD;
*ever loyal
to Moss High*

Donald Burns, Sr., 63, HUD;
*taught and coached kids
for nineteen years*

**Karen Gist Carr, 32,
Army Recruiting;**
*could make anyone
love aerobics*

Michael Joe Carrillo, 44, FHA,
*dubbed "the Fifth Beatle"
because he loved the Fab Four*

Rona Linn Chafey, 35, DEA;
*"The type of person who kept
the drawer full of candy,"
says her ex-boss*

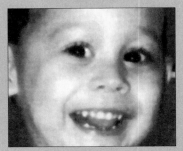

Zackary Chavez, 3;
*mother wanted his grave
to be close enough
for her to visit every day*

**Robert Chipman, 51, Water
Resources Board;**
*"A prince of a guy,"
says a friend*

Kimberly Clark, 39, HUD;
*her wedding day was to be
the Saturday after she died*

**Anthony Christopher
Cooper II, 2½;**
*"This little boy could do no
wrong," says his grandfather*

**Antonio Ansara Cooper Jr.,
six months;**
*just learning to crawl
and say "Da-da"*

Dana Cooper, 24, America's Kids;
*"Everything she did, she did
for the children,"
says her husband*

Harley Cottingham, 46, DOD;
*had just planted
six hundred Christmas trees*

Kim Cousins, 33, HUD;
homeroom mom
at Steed Elementary

Aaron Coverdale, 5½;
loved to go for a truck ride
with his father
and brother, Elijah

Elijah Coverdale, 2½; *after the*
bombing, his father walked the
streets with his sons' photos,
asking, "Have you seen them?"

Jaci Rae Coyne, 14 months;
loved to have
her picture taken

Kathy Cregan, 60, Social Security;
spoiled her grandsons
and her Yorkshire terriers

Richard Cummins, 55, USDA;
dedicated his career
to the care of animals

Steven Curry, 44, GSA;
hunter, fisherman,
Baptist church deacon

Sgt. Benjamin Davis, 29,
Marine Recruiting;
father of Vandrea Aileen, 1

Diana Day, 36, HUD;
"She was the laughter
of our family,"
says her brother, Bill

Peter DeMaster, 44, DOD;
an Eagle Scout
in every way

Castine Deveroux, 49, HUD;
often spoke of her faith

Sheila Driver, 28,
Credit Union customer;
expectant mother

Tylor Eaves, 8 months;
*"He could get anything
he wanted from us,"*
says his grandmother

Ashley Megan Eckles, 4½,
Social Security customer;
*getting a song all ready
for the Oklahoma Opry*

Susan Jane Ferrell, 37, HUD;
*advocate for Native Americans;
loved all dancing, from
ballet to belly*

Chip Fields, 48, DEA;
*had just told her mother,
"I'm happy with my life"*

Katherine Ann Finley, 44,
Credit Union;
*worked her way up
from teller to vice-president*

Judy Fisher, 45, HUD;
*she'd been shopping for things
to go with the renovation
of their house*

Linda Florence, 43, HUD;
*wife for sixteen years,
mother for eighteen months*

Donald Fritzler, 64,
Social Security customer;
architect

Mary Anne Fritzler, 57,
Social Security customer;
*married to Donald
for thirty-five years and one day*

Tevin Garrett, 1½;
*loved to ride
his Lion King bike*

Laura Garrison, 65,
Social Security customer;
*"She will always be here,"
write her three children*

Jamie Lee Genzer, 32,
Credit Union;
*sang in a chorus
called the Sweet Adelines*

**Margaret Goodson, 54,
Social Security;**
confirmed motorcyclist

**Kevin "Lee" Gottshall II,
6 months;**
a.k.a. "Sweet Pea"

**Ethel Griffin, 55,
Social Security;**
*"My perfect partner in life,"
writes her husband, Bruce*

**Capt. Randy Guzman, 28,
Marine Recruiting;**
*led infantry
in Persian Gulf War*

**Cheryl Bradley Hammons, 44,
Social Security customer;**
*nurse at Four Seasons
Nursing Home*

**Ronald Harding, 55,
Social Security;**
*good on clarinet, sax, flute,
violin, and cello*

**Thomas Hawthorne Sr., 52,
Social Security customer;**
*often surprised his wife
with chocolate-covered cherries*

Adele Higginbottom, 44, USDA;
*secretary of local chapter
of Federal Employed Women*

**Anita Hightower, 27,
Job Corps;**
*came to Oklahoma City
to care for sick aunt*

Gene Hodges Jr., 54, HUD;
*"He will always be missed
and never forgotten,"
writes his wife*

**Peggy Holland, 37,
Army Recruiting;**
*taught summer Bible school
at Knob Hill Baptist Church*

**Linda Colleen Housley, 53,
Credit Union;**
*hobbies were making stuffed
animals and collecting clowns*

George Howard, 46, HUD;
*had just moved from California
to be near his widowed father*

**Wanda Lee Howell, 34,
America's Kids;**
*always carried a Bible
in her purse*

Robbin Huff, 37, Credit Union;
*her first child
was due in June*

**Dr. Charles Hurlburt, 73,
Social Security customer;**
*medical missionary,
married forty-five years to Jean*

**Jean Hurlburt, 67,
Social Security customer;**
nurse

**Paul Ice, 43,
Customs Service;**
*one of the first special agents
assigned to Oklahoma City*

Christi Jenkins, 33, Credit Union;
*"Her life was her children
and her church,"
says her pastor*

Norma Jean Johnson, 62, DOD;
a horse-show regular

Raymond Johnson, 59;
*volunteer at Social Security
for the Older Native American
Program*

Larry Jones, 46, FHA;
*"A great friend, a super
husband, but mostly a loving
father," writes his wife, Karen*

**Alvin Justes, 54,
Credit Union customer;**
Vietnam veteran

**Blake Ryan Kennedy,
18 months;**
*always saying
hello and goodbye*

Carole Sue Khalil, 50, USDA;
great eye for detail

Valerie Jo Koelsch, 33,
Credit Union;
didn't throw like a girl

Carolyn Kreymborg, 57, HUD;
loved all flowers,
particularly azaleas

Teresa Lea Lauderdale, 41, HUD;
widowed mother
of two teenage sons

Kathy Leinen, 47,
Credit Union;
always doing crafts
with her husband, Henry

Carrie Ann Lenz, 26, DEA;
six months pregnant
with Michael James Lenz III

Donald Leonard, 50,
Secret Service;
"a kindhearted giant of a man"
who protected seven presidents

Airman First Class
Lakesha Levy, 21,
Social Security customer;
a natural comedian

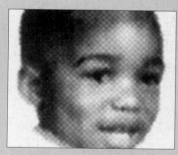
Dominique London, 2½;
a mischief-maker—
liked to turn off the speaker
while the pastor preached

Rheta Long, 60, USDA;
avid fan
of Jewel Box Theater
productions

Michael Loudenslager, 48, GSA;
a modern-day cowboy

Donna Luster, 43,
Social Security customer;
mother of six

**Robert Lee Luster Jr., 45,
Social Security customer;
*father of six,
facing eviction***

**Mickey Maroney, 50,
Secret Service;** *piped
"On the Road Again" through
Ted Kennedy's campaign plane*

**Brenda Daniels Marsh, 42,
America's Kids;**
*children were the focus
of her life*

J.K. Martin, 34, FHA;
*kept every note his wife, Diane,
ever gave him*

**Rev. Gilberto Martinez, 45,
Social Security customer;**
*youngest child, Gilberto,
is 2 months old*

James McCarthy, 53, HUD;
*in Oklahoma
only four months*

Kenneth McCullough, 36, DEA;
Patrick and Jessica's dad

Betsy McGonnell, 47, HUD;
*a single mother
of two*

**Linda McKinney, 47,
Secret Service;**
*enjoyed fishing "if I baited the
hook for her," her husband says*

**Airman First Class Cartney Jean
McRaven, 19,
Social Security customer;**
just home from Haiti

**Claude Medearis, 42,
Customs Service;**
*recently promoted
to senior special-agent-in-charge*

**Claudette Meek, 43,
Credit Union;**
bubbly, outgoing, and spiritual

Frankie Ann Merrell, 23,
Credit Union;
mother of Morgan Taylor, 2½

Derwin Miller, 27,
Social Security;
was Alpha Phi Alpha
at University of Arkansas

Leigh Mitchell, 64;
Social Security customer;
always feeding the birds
around her home

John Clayton Moss III, 45,
Army Recruiting;
"He had found his niche,"
his sister says

Trish Nix, 47, HUD;
avid antiques collector

Jerry Lee Parker, 45, FHA;
loved woodworking,
collecting antiques

Jill Randolph, 27,
Credit Union;
loved church
and her cat, Rascal

Michelle Ann Reeder, 33, FHA;
an avid gardener,
like her mother,
Carolyn Kreymborg

Terry Smith Rees, 41, HUD;
collected teddy bears

Mary Rentie, 39, HUD;
expert quilter
and seamstress

Antonio Reyes, 55, HUD;
active in
the Hispanic community

Kathryn Ridley, 24,
student reporting to Job Corps;
a budding artist; most of her
sketches were lost with her

Trudy Rigney, 32,
Water Resources Board;
two weeks
from college graduation

Claudine Ritter, 48, Credit Union;
"God bless, Claudine," writes
her brother. "We're so sorry
you had to be in this book."

Christy Rosas, 22, Credit Union;
"Until we meet again, honey,"
writes her husband,
"I love you"

Sonja Sanders, 27,
Credit Union;
working toward
a banking degree

Lanny Scroggins, 46, HUD;
loved music, cars,
and playing ball
with his two boys

Kathy Lynn Seidl, 39,
Secret Service;
wife of Glenn,
mother of Clint, age 7

Leora Lee Sells, 57, HUD;
hit almost every
U. of Oklahoma home game
in almost every sport

Karan Shepherd, 27,
Credit Union;
youngest loan officer
ever appointed

Chase Smith, 3;
"When we got to day care,"
his mother writes, "Chase
would jump out of the car"

Colton Smith, 2;
"Colton always wanted me
to hold him,"
says his mother

Master Sgt. Victoria Sohn, 36;
at work, a perfectionist;
at home, a mother of five

John Thomas Stewart, 51, HUD;
easygoing, with three children
and a love of horses

**Dolores Stratton, 52,
Army Recruiting;**
*"I told her I loved her and to
drive safely," says her husband*

**Emilio Tapia, 49,
Social Security customer;**
*his son, Manuel, came from
Mexico to take his father home*

Victoria Texter, 37, Credit Union;
*maker of
porcelain dolls*

**Charlotte Thomas, 43,
Social Security;**
*produced Black Awareness
program for several years*

**Michael Thompson, 47,
Social Security;**
*painter, musician, animal lover,
amateur builder*

**Virginia Thompson, 56,
Credit Union;**
*brought up three children
on her own*

Kayla Marie Titsworth, 3;
*visiting dad's new office
at Army Recruiting*

**Rick Tomlin, 46,
Transportation Dept.;**
*equal parts Republican, car
collector, and John Lennon fan*

**LaRue Treanor, 55,
Social Security customer;**
*married thirty-five years
to Luther*

**Luther Treanor, 61,
Social Security customer;**
*spent only one day of his
marriage apart from his wife*

Larry Turner, 42, DOD;
*loved playing clarinet
in the St. John Baptist Church*

Jules Valdez, 51, HUD;
*Rotary Club,
every Wednesday at noon*

John Karl VanEss III, 67, HUD;
"When I die," he always said,
"plant a tree
and throw a party"

Johnny Wade, 45, FHA;
"I still can't believe that
Johnny won't be coming
home," writes his wife, Jeannie

Bob Walker Jr., 52, Social Security;
"He loved his computer second
only to his family,"
writes his wife, Judith

David Walker, 54, HUD;
"He never hung up the phone
without saying 'I love you,'"
says his wife, Janet

Wanda Watkins, 49,
Army Recruiting;
renowned for
her crocheted doilies

Michael Weaver, 45, HUD;
a great, dry wit,
but couldn't sing,
unless it was an old song

Julie Marie Welch, 23,
Social Security;
Marquette University,
Class of '94

Robert Westberry, 57, DOD;
"totally dedicated to his family,"
said his daughter, Sue

Alan Whicher, 40,
Secret Service;
his funeral was attended
by his ex-boss, Bill Clinton

JoAnn Whittenberg, 35, HUD;
"God broke our heart to
prove He only takes the best,"
writes her family

Frances Williams, 48, HUD;
she had a real sweet tooth

Scott Williams, 24,
making a delivery;
left a wife and an unborn
daughter, Kylie

**W. Stephen Williams, 42,
Social Security;
played guitar in the garage**

**Clarence Wilson, 49, HUD;
chief legal counsel and former
councilman from Forest Park**

**Sharon Wood-Chesnut, 47,
Social Security;
Christ Lutheran Church's
volunteer for children**

**Ronota Woodbridge, 31, FHA;
her family church in Akansas has
named a garden for her**

**Tresia Jo Worton, 28,
Credit Union;
"A beautiful girl, just like her
picture," says her cousin**

**Buddy Youngblood, 62, FHA;
"It was probably love at first
sight," says Kathy, his wife
of twenty-one years**

Calvin Battle

Peola Y. Battle

Andrea Blanton

Lola Bolden

Peggy Clark

Juretta Guiles

169

By Governor Frank Keating and First Lady Cathy Keating

EPILOGUE

This book is an act of love. It was created by and for Oklahomans, as our gift to America. We present it as our thank-you note to the world.

Within hours of the terrible explosion at the Alfred P. Murrah Federal Building on April 19, 1995, amid sorrow and grief and uncertainty and horror, flowers began to bloom on the fences and sidewalks near the still-smoking building. They were drawn and painted by children, and over the next two weeks, as the deadly search for victims continued, our city and state blossomed. Hardened disaster-assistance teams from faraway places were amazed at our spirit. They were overwhelmed by our hospitality. As we suffered through the most devastating tragedy in Oklahoma's history, we continued to display the strength and dignity and courage—and the warmth—that is Oklahoma.

One of the visiting search-and-rescue workers said, "Oklahoma is the best-kept secret in America." Another, as he left, pulled a dollar bill from his pocket and waved it. "See this bill, Governor?" he said. "It's an Oklahoma dollar. It's the dollar I arrived with and it's the dollar I'm leaving with. Nobody would let me spend it."

Those visitors helped write this book. Just as they mingled their tears with ours during the awful search-and-rescue operation, they now add their words to our own to tell the story of a tragedy beyond imagining; of the triumphant response of a city and a state; of America's arms opened wide to embrace all of us in a time of terrible need.

Most of the stories are those of Oklahomans— the survivors and the families, the rescuers and the helpers, the witnesses and those we lost—told in the words of those who lived them. There are special stories of children, of heroism, of compassion and love. There are no stories of hate. Oklahomans have had enough of hate and its deadly outriders.

From the beginning the book was intended to raise vital funds for Project Recovery OKC, Inc. The fund will assist with funeral, medical, counseling, living, and educational expenses incurred by the hundreds of families most directly involved in the tragedy. The needs of these families will continue for years to come. Volunteers stepped forward from everywhere to help with the project. The Oklahoma City Police and Fire departments, the Army and Air National Guard, state and municipal agencies, the Federal Emer-

gency Management Agency, private firms, news organizations—all volunteered their time and pictures, at no cost. This is the most complete account of what happened in Oklahoma on April 19 and in the weeks that followed. It comes from the collective heart of our state. Although it is not possible to name the thousands of volunteers who helped Oklahoma overcome tragedy—or even the hundreds who played a role in preparing this volume—we must pay special tribute to the men and women of the Oklahoma City Police and Fire departments and the emergency medical services of our community. They were the first—and last— on the scene. They risked all to save others. One nurse, Rebecca Anderson, died saving life.

We must also thank the staff of *The Daily Oklahoman*, led by the managing editor, Ed Kelley. Publisher Edward L. Gaylord detailed staff members to assist us and agreed to lend his newspaper's photo and text archive to this project. It was the single largest archival record available on the bombing and its aftermath.

It is impossible to thank the tens of thousands of Americans who have written us since the tragedy. Millions more have sent their prayers and thoughts—not as tangible as a letter or card, but equally real and equally appreciated. During the televised prayer service on April 23, we felt the world watching and praying and reaching out to toughen our hearts. We return that love with this volume.

In the end, this is not just Oklahoma's story, but America's as well. During the darkest days of late April, we received two letters that told us much about our nation and our people. One, from a Vietnam veteran, included his Purple Heart. He asked that we present it to the parents of a murdered child. The second, from a small child, enfolded a stuffed dog. Give this to someone who needs it, she said—someone who needs it more than me. That is America. With gratitude and love, with hope and deep appreciation, we proudly present Oklahoma's story to you.

The Project Recovery OKC, Inc., fund is administered by a citizens' committee under the auspices of the Office of the Governor and the Office of the Mayor of Oklahoma City. Individuals or corporations are encouraged to contribute. **The fund's address is P.O. Box 850234, Oklahoma City, OK 73185-0234. For credit-card contributions by VISA or MASTERCARD, please call the Office of the Governor at (800) 518-3601.**

MY GRATITUDE

Our thanks go, first of all, to those who told us their stories: the survivors of the explosion, the public safety workers who rushed to help them; the families of those who died; the volunteers. They are heroes and heroines without number. Our goal was to memorialize their experiences with truth. I believe we have succeeded.

A special thanks to Random House. Alberto Vitale, Harold Evans, Clive Irving, Angela Buchanan, and the rest of the New York team set a record as the book moved from concept to production in little more than six weeks. Clive and Angela made urgent trips to Oklahoma City early in the process. They are now honorary Okies. So are the executives at Random House, who decided from day one that every dime of profit from this book would go to help the victims.

In Oklahoma, Mike Brake, chief writer in the Office of the Governor, continued his regular duties and also coordinated the task of gathering personal accounts and photos. Nine volunteer editors abandoned their families and jobs to immerse themselves in this immense tragedy. They met with families and survivors and rescuers, seeking their stories, then edited the steady flood of material for daily shipment to New York. For two weeks, a hastily assembled team produced the equivalent of a daily newspaper every twenty-four hours.

Taprina Milburn and Micah Swafford brought sensitivity to the task of contacting the families of the 168 Oklahomans killed on April 19. Paul Meyers sat for hours in fire stations recording the recollections of the first firefighters on the scene. Allison Thompson earned honorary Oklahoma City Police badges for her two small sons, who often accompanied her as she tracked the stories of law enforcement officers. Jan Vassar read and edited the frightening and often uplifting tales of the blast survivors, many of whom still bore fresh wounds and stitches. Jim Ross searched nationwide for the stories of FEMA task force members, touching area codes from Florida to California. Deborah Bouziden chased the volunteers—the Red Cross and Salvation Army workers and the pastors. Jan May solicited the astonishing tales of the medical workers. Suzie Quinton worked the military beat and also unearthed the powerful and previously unknown story of Michael Loudenslager, the unsung hero.

The Oklahoma editors worked as volunteers. Daily they read and listened to the raw, often tearful, accounts of people who had only recently suffered amazing trauma. It is a measure of their professionalism that from a total of twelve hundred individual accounts gathered, they prepared more than five hundred for publication; it is a tribute to their humanity that they often had to stop and weep. Suzie Quinton symbolized the dignity and caring attitude of Oklahoma's volunteer writers and editors when she interviewed a widowed mother of five, turned in her story...and took the entire family to the zoo.

Patti Rosenfeld not only introduced me to the Random House executives who first opened the door to this project, she also undertook the difficult and sensitive task of seeking permission from 168 bereaved families to publish the photos of those who were lost. She became at once a skilled detective and a compassionate counselor.

To the Reverend Billy Graham, a special word of appreciation. Not only did he rush to Oklahoma City in the first days after the tragedy, he contributed the book's heartfelt foreword. He is a national treasure and a true friend of Oklahoma.

Finally, a special note of thanks to Governor Frank Keating—my husband. In the awful days and nights after April 19 you stood before the world as a symbol of Oklahoma's spirit. It was my privilege to share your dignity in public and your tears in private.

—CATHY KEATING

THE STAFF

This book was produced by staff drawn from Random House and Condé Nast Publications in New York. The editor would like to thank those who helped provide support and resources with unstinting generosity:

CONDÉ NAST PUBLICATIONS
Pamela M. Van Zandt, Executive Vice-President; Thomas J. Wallace;
Gloria Kessler; Harry Wachenheim
Computer services: Alex McDonald; Thuy-An Julien
RANDOM HOUSE
Walter Weintz; Della Mancuso; Ivan Held; Ruth Fecych; Irina Woelfle
Editorial staff: Angela Buchanan; Tish Durkin
Art production: W. Mitchell Wells; David Shay
Graphics: Carl Gude, John Tomanio, Alex Reardon
Photo research: Kathleen Kiley
Still-life photography: Chris Bierlien
Copy: Veronica Windholz
Editorial intern: Elisabeth Costa de Beauregard

PHOTO CREDITS

Special thanks to Jim Argo of The Daily Oklahoman and all the agencies and photographers who donated their material.
Page 8: captions read left column top to bottom, middle column top to bottom, right column top to bottom. Jim Argo/Daily Oklahoman; ©1995 Hi-Shots International; ©1995 Hi-Shots International; ©1995 Hi-Shots International; June Ranney; June Ranney; SSGT. Kimmy Tucker/Oklahoma Air National Guard; SSGT. Kimmy Tucker/Oklahoma Air National Guard; June Ranney; ©1995 Hi-Shots International; Paul Hellstern/Daily Oklahoman; Monica Almeida/The New York Times; SSGT. Chasteen/Oklahoma Air National Guard; pages 10–11: Courtesy, Western History Collections, University of Oklahoma Library; page 12: Courtesy, Howard Robson; page 13: Courtesy, Western History Collections, University of Oklahoma Library; pages 14–15: Courtesy, Western History Collections, University of Oklahoma Library; pages 16–17: Courtesy, The Oakland Museum; page 18: A.Y. Owen/LIFE Magazine ©TIME Inc.; page 19: Courtesy, Western History Collections, University of Oklahoma Library; pages 20–21: Wil Moore/Ace Aerial Photo Inc.; pages 28–29: KFOR-TV/Cable News Network/via AP; pages 30–31: Richard Hail; page 32: Christian Coy and Cottrell Dawson/Sipa Press; page 33: Steve Sisney/Daily Oklahoman; pages 36–37: Jim Argo/Daily Oklahoman; page 39: Lee Kuhlman; pages 42–43: Steve Sisney/Daily Oklahoman; page 45: AP/Wide World Photos; page 46: Top: Jim Argo/Daily Oklahoman; Bottom: Steve Gooch/Daily Oklahoman; page 47: Top and Bottom: Steve Sisney/Daily Oklahoman; pages 48–49: Steve Sisney/Daily Oklahoman; page 50: Jim Argo/Daily Oklahoman; page 54: Steve Gooch/Daily Oklahoman; page 55: Mike Simons/Daily Oklahoman; page 58: Lester Bob LaRue/Sygma; pages 62–63: Steve Sisney/Daily Oklahoman; page 66: Roger Klock/Daily Oklahoman; page 69: Paul Hellstern/Daily Oklahoman; pages 70–71: Steve Sisney/Daily Oklahoman/SABA; pages 72–73: Larry L. Smith/Tinker Air Force Base, Oklahoma; pages 74–75: Ron Jenkins/Ft. Worth Star Telegram/Sipa Press; page 77: ©1995 Hi-Shots International; pages 80–81: SSGT. Kimmy Tucker/Oklahoma Air National Guard; pages 82–83: Wil Moore/Ace Aerial Photo Inc; page 91: F.B.I.; pages 92–93: David McDaniel/Daily Oklahoman; page 95: Paul Moseley/Ft. Worth Star Telegram/Sipa Press; pages 96–97: Lana Jeanne Tyree; pages 98–99: SSGT. Kimmy Tucker/Oklahoma Air National Guard; pages 100–101: David McDaniel/Daily Oklahoman; page 103: AP/Wide World Photos; pages 104–105: Roger Klock/Daily Oklahoman; pages 106–115: David Modell/Katz/SABA; pages 118–119: David Modell/Katz/SABA; pages 120–121: Brad Markel/Gamma-Liaison; pages 122–123: Jim Argo/Daily Oklahoman; page 124: Steve Liss/TIME Magazine; page 126: Steve Sisney/Daily Oklahoman; page 135: Mike Simons/Daily Oklahoman; pages 136–137: Steve Liss/Gamma-Liaison; page 138: Top left, Bottom left, Bottom right: Jim Argo/Daily Oklahoman; Top right: Mike Simons/Daily Oklahoman; page 139: Top left, Bottom right: Jim Argo/Daily Oklahoman; Top right, Bottom left: Mike Simons/Daily Oklahoman; pages 140–141: Blake Sell/Reuters; page 143: David Modell/Katz/SABA; pages 144–145: Allen Rose/Ft.Worth Star Telegram/Sipa Press; page 146: Tom Salyer/PEOPLE Weekly ©1995; page 147: Jim Argo/Daily Oklahoman; pages 148–149: Steve Sisney/Daily Oklahoman; pages 150–151: SSGT. Kimmy Tucker/Oklahoma Air National Guard; page 176: George R. Wilson/Daily Oklahoman.

MAKING IT HAPPEN

This book will substantially assist the relief fund for the families of the victims of the Oklahoma City bombing, in large part because of the spontaneous generosity of the companies identified below. Their contribution is gratefully acknowledged.

The inspiration for this project came initially from Governor Keating and First Lady Cathy Keating of Oklahoma, and Random House was honored to be their publisher. It was our wish to produce and publish the book without charging any overhead so that the fund would benefit from the profits to the fullest possible extent. Random House vendors responded in the same spirit, making no charge for their supplies and services, therefore contributing significantly to the profit.

The book was planned, written, and produced in little more than six weeks, with energetic assistance at all levels from *The Daily Oklahoman*. Condé Nast Publications supplied resources and offices.

The thanks of all concerned to:

Printing and Binding donated by R.R. Donnelley & Sons Company, Willard, Ohio, corporate headquarters, Chicago, Illinois

Spine cloth provided by Industrial Coatings, Inc., Chicago

Side Panel Material donated by Permalin Products, Co., New York

Case decorating foil donated by General Roll Leaf, Long Island City, New York

Portion of paper donated by Northwest Division of Potlatch Corporation and the Allan & Gray Division of the Alling & Cory Company

Portion of paper donated by International Paper, Coated Papers Division

Portion of paper donated by Stora, World Class Manufacturer of Coated Free Sheet Papers

Portion of paper donated by Lindenmeyr Book Publishing Papers

Portion of paper donated by Westvaco Corporation

Film lamination donated by GBC Film Products, 712 West Winthrop Ave., Addison, IL 60101

Jacket prep, printing and finishing donated by Coral Graphic Services, Inc., 840 South Broadway, Hicksville, NY 11801

Color separations and film work by North Market Street Graphics, Lancaster, PA

Jacket paper donated by Websource. "We at Websource offer our deepest condolences to the families and friends of the victims."

Endsheet material provided by RIS Paper Company, Long Island City, New York, and Union Camp Corporation, Wayne, New Jersey

"EL-HI" board provided by Rock-Tenn Paperboard Products, Otsega, Michigan

Tapecraft has conjoined with Gane in supplying the headbands for the "Oklahoma Relief Project."

Cartons donated by Mid-States Container Corporation and Box USA

And thanks to Planned Television Arts for donating a radio drive time tour and a print teleconference.

Alfred P. Murrah Building: opened October 1977; imploded May 1995

LUCIO ALEMAN Jr • TERESA ALEXANDER • RICHARD ALLEN • TED ALLEN • BAYLEE ALMON • DIANE ALTHOUSE • REBE
ANDERSON • PAMELA ARGO • SANDY AVERY • PETER AVILLANOZA • CALVIN BATTLE • PEOLA Y. BATTLE • DANIELLE NICOLE BE
OLETA BIDDY • SHELLY TURNER BLAND • ANDREA BLANTON • OLEN BLOOMER • LOLA BOLDEN • JAMES BOLES • MARK BOL
CASSANDRA BOOKER • CAROL BOWERS • PEACHLYN BRADLEY • WOODY BRADY • CYNTHIA BROWN • PAUL BROXTERMAN • GABR
BRUCE • KIMBERLY BURGESS • DAVID BURKETT • DONALD BURNS • KAREN GIST CARR • MICHAEL JOE CARRILLO • R
LINN CHAFEY • ZACKARY CHAVEZ • ROBERT CHIPMAN • KIMBERLY CLARK • PEGGY CLARK • ANTHONY CHRISTOP
COOPER II • ANTONIO ANSARA COOPER Jr • DANA COOPER • HARLEY COTTINGHAM • KIM COUSINS • AARON COVERDALE • EL
COVERDALE • JACI RAE COYNE • KATHY CREGAN • RICHARD CUMMINS • STEVEN CURRY • BENJAMIN DAVIS • DIANA DAY • PE
DeMASTER • CASTINE DEVEROUX • SHEILA DRIVER • TYLOR EAVES • ASHLEY MEGAN ECKLES • SUSAN JANE FERRELL • CHIP FIE
KATHERINE FINLEY • JUDY FISHER • LINDA FLORENCE • DONALD FRITZLER • MARY ANNE FRITZLER • TEVIN GARRETT • L
GARRISON • JAMIE GENZER • MARGARET GOODSON • KEVIN "LEE" GOTTSHALL II • ETHEL GRIFFIN • JURETTA GUILES • RA
GUZMAN • CHERYL BRADLEY HAMMONS • RONALD HARDING • THOMAS HAWTHORNE Sr • ADELE HIGGINBOTTOM • A
HIGHTOWER • GENE HODGES Jr • PEGGY HOLLAND • COLLEEN HOUSLEY • GEORGE HOWARD • WANDA LEE HOWELL • ROBBIN H
CHARLES HURLBURT • JEAN HURLBURT • PAUL DOUGLAS ICE • CHRISTI JENKINS • NORMA JEAN JOHNSON • RAYMOND JOHNS
LARRY JONES | • ALVIN JUSTES • BLAKE RYAN KENNEDY • CAROLE SUE KHALIL • VALERIE JO KOELSCH • CARC
KREYMBORG • TERESA LEA LAUDERDALE • KATHY LEINEN • CARRIE ANN LENZ • DONALD LEONARD • LAKESHA LEVY • DOMIN
LONDON • RHETA LONG • MICHAEL LOUDENSLAGER • DONNA LUSTER • ROBERT LEE LUSTER Jr • MICKEY MARONEY • BRE
DANIELS MARSH • J.K. MARTIN • GILBERTO MARTINEZ • JAMES McCARTHY • KENNETH McCULLOUGH • BETSY McGONNELL • L
McKINNEY • CARTNEY JEAN McRAVEN • CLAUDE MEDEARIS • CLAUDETTE MEEK • FRANKIE ANN MERRELL • DERWIN WADE MIL
LEIGH MITCHELL • JOHN CLAYTON MOSS III • TRISH NIX • JERRY LEE PARKER • JILL RANDOLPH • MICHELLE ANN REEDER • T
SMITH REES • MARY RENTIE • ANTONIO REYES • KATHRYN RIDLEY • TRUDY RIGNEY • CLAUDINE RITTER • CHRISTY ROS
SONJA SANDERS • LANNY SCROGGINS • KATHY LYNN SEIDL • LEORA LEE SELLS • KARAN SHEPHERD • CHASE SMITH • CO
SMITH • VICTORIA SOHN • JOHN THOMAS STEWART • DOLORES STRATTON • EMILIO TAPIA • VICTORIA TEXTER • CHARL
THOMAS • MICHAEL THOMPSON • VIRGINIA THOMPSON • KAYLA MARIE TITSWORTH • RICK TOMLIN • LARUE TREANOR • LU
TREANOR • LARRY TURNER • JULES VALDEZ • JOHN KARL VANESS III • JOHNNY WADE • BOB WALKER Jr • DAVID WALKER • WA
WATKINS • MICHAEL WEAVER • JULIE MARIE WELCH • ROBERT WESTBERRY • ALAN WHICHER • JOANN WHITTENBERG • FRA
WILLIAMS • SCOTT WILLIAMS • W. STEPHEN WILLIAMS • CLARENCE WILSON • SHARON WOOD-CHESNUT • RONOTA WOODBRI
TRESIA JO WORTON • JOHN YOUNGBLOOD • LUCIO ALEMAN Jr • TERESA ALEXANDER • RICHARD ALLEN • TED ALLEN • BA
ALMON • DIANE ALTHOUSE • REBECCA ANDERSON • PAMELA ARGO • SANDY AVERY • PETER AVILLANOZA • CALVIN BATTLE • PEO
BATTLE • DANIELLE NICOLE BELL • OLETA BIDDY • SHELLY TURNER BLAND • ANDREA BLANTON • OLEN BLOOMER • LOLA BOL
JAMES BOLES • MARK BOLTE • CASSANDRA BOOKER • CAROL BOWERS • PEACHLYN BRADLEY • WOODY BRADY • CYNTHIA BRO
PAUL BROXTERMAN • GABREON BRUCE • KIMBERLY BURGESS • DAVID BURKETT • DONALD BURNS • KAREN
CARR • MICHAEL JOE CARRILLO • RONA LINN CHAFEY • ZACKARY CHAVEZ • ROBERT CHIPMAN • KIMBERLY CLARK • PEGGY CL
ANTHONY CHRISTOPHER COOPER II • ANTONIO ANSARA COOPER Jr • DANA COOPER • HARLEY COTTINGHAM • KIM COUS
AARON COVERDALE • ELIJAH COVERDALE • JACI RAE COYNE • KATHY CREGAN • RICHARD CUMMINS • STEVEN CURRY • BENJ
DAVIS • DIANA DAY • PETER DeMASTER • CASTINE DEVEROUX • SHEILA DRIVER • TYLOR EAVES • ASHLEY MEGAN ECKLES • S
JANE FERRELL • CHIP FIELDS • KATHERINE FINLEY • JUDY FISHER • LINDA FLORENCE • DONALD FRITZLER • MARY ANNE FRITZ
TEVIN GARRETT • LAURA GARRISON • JAMIE GENZER • MARGARET GOODSON • KEVIN "LEE" GOTTSHALL II • ETHEL GRIF
JURETTA GUILES • RANDY GUZMAN • CHERYL BRADLEY HAMMONS • RONALD HARDING • THOMAS HAWTHORNE Sr • A
HIGGINBOTTOM • ANITA HIGHTOWER • GENE HODGES Jr • PEGGY HOLLAND • COLLEEN HOUSLEY • GEORGE HOWARD • WAND
HOWELL • ROBBIN HUFF • CHARLES HURLBURT • JEAN HURLBURT • PAUL DOUGLAS ICE • CHRISTI JENKINS • NORMA JEAN JOHN
RAYMOND JOHNSON • LARRY JONES • ALVIN JUSTES • BLAKE RYAN KENNEDY • CAROLE SUE KHALIL • VALERIE JO KOELS
CAROLYN KREYMBORG • TERESA LEA LAUDERDALE • KATHY LEINEN • CARRIE ANN LENZ • DONALD LEONARD • LAK
LEVY • DOMINIQUE LONDON • RHETA LONG • MICHAEL LOUDENSLAGER • DONNA LUSTER • ROBERT LEE LUSTER Jr • M
MARONEY • BRENDA DANIELS MARSH • J.K. MARTIN • GILBERTO MARTINEZ • JAMES McCARTHY • KENNETH McCULLOUGH •
McGONNELL • LINDA McKINNEY • CARTNEY JEAN McRAVEN • CLAUDE MEDEARIS • CLAUDETTE MEEK • FRANKIE ANN MER
DERWIN WADE MILLER • LEIGH MITCHELL • JOHN CLAYTON MOSS III • TRISH NIX • JERRY LEE PARKER • JILL RANDO
MICHELLE ANN REEDER • TERRY SMITH REES • MARY RENTIE • ANTONIO REYES • KATHRYN RIDLEY • TRUDY RIGNEY • CLAU
RITTER • CHRISTY ROSAS • SONJA SANDERS • LANNY SCROGGINS • KATHY LYNN SEIDL • LEORA LEE SELLS • KARAN SHEPH
CHASE SMITH • COLTON SMITH • VICTORIA SOHN • JOHN THOMAS STEWART • DOLORES STRATTON • EMILIO TAPIA • VIC
TEXTER • CHARLOTTE THOMAS • MICHAEL THOMPSON • VIRGINIA THOMPSON • KAYLA MARIE TITSWORTH • RICK TOMLIN • L
TREANOR • LUTHER TREANOR • LARRY TURNER • JULES VALDEZ • JOHN KARL VANESS III • JOHNNY WADE • BOB WALKER Jr •
WALKER • WANDA WATKINS • MICHAEL WEAVER • JULIE MARIE WELCH • ROBERT WESTBERRY • ALAN WHICHER • J
WHITTENBERG • FRANCES WILLIAMS • SCOTT WILLIAMS • W. STEPHEN WILLIAMS • CLARENCE WILSON • SHARON WOOD-CHES
RONOTA WOODBRIDGE • TRESIA JO WORTON • JOHN YOUNGBLOOD • LUCIO ALEMAN Jr • TERESA ALEXANDER • RIC
ALLEN • TED ALLEN • BAYLEE ALMON • DIANE ALTHOUSE • REBECCA ANDERSON • PAMELA ARGO • SANDY AVERY •
AVILLANOZA • CALVIN BATTLE • PEOLA Y. BATTLE • DANIELLE NICOLE BELL • OLETA BIDDY • SHELLY TURNER BLAND • AN
BLANTON • OLEN BLOOMER • LOLA BOLDEN • JAMES BOLES • MARK BOLTE • CASSANDRA BOOKER • CAROL BOWERS • PEAC
BRADLEY • WOODY BRADY • CYNTHIA BROWN • PAUL BROXTERMAN • GABREON BRUCE • KIMBERLY BURGESS • DAVID BURK
DONALD BURNS • KAREN GIST CARR • MICHAEL JOE CARRILLO • RONA LINN CHAFEY • ZACKARY CHAVEZ • ROBERT CHIP
KIMBERLY CLARK • PEGGY CLARK • ANTHONY CHRISTOPHER COOPER II • ANTONIO ANSARA COOPER Jr • DANA COOPER •
COTTINGHAM • KIM COUSINS • AARON COVERDALE • ELIJAH COVERDALE • JACI RAE COYNE • KATHY CREGAN • K